# *Molly Parkin*
# A Bit between the Teeth

*Sandwich recipes by*
*Topsy Fyers*

WARD LOCK LIMITED · LONDON

*First published in 1985 by Ward Lock Ltd,*
*82 Gower Street, London WC1E 6EQ*
*Designed and produced by*
*The Rainbird Publishing Group Ltd,*
*40 Park Street, London W1Y 4DE*



*Photographs by John Timbers*
*Typeset by Bookworm Typesetting Ltd, Manchester*
*Colour reproduction by Adroit Photolitho Ltd, Birmingham*
*Printed and bound by Toppan, Singapore*

**British Library Cataloguing in Publication Data**

*Parkin, Molly*
*A bit between the teeth.*
*1. Sandwiches*
*I. Title*
*641.8'4 TX818*

*ISBN 0-7063-6401-5*

# CONTENTS


| | |
|---|---|
| *Introduction by Molly* | 4 |
| *Bread by Topsy* | 12 |
| *Tots at Tea Time* | 24 |
| *Hamper for Open-air Theatres* | 32 |
| *Office Lunch Box* | 40 |
| *Point to Point* | 48 |
| *Non-Carnivores* | 56 |
| *Gap Stoppers* | 64 |
| *Tea at the Ritz* | 72 |
| *Twelfth August* | 76 |
| *Director's Working Lunch* | 84 |
| *And so to Bed* | 93 |
| *Index* | 95 |

# Introduction by Molly

*For someone like me now, a self-confessed, salivating sandwich addict, it seems strange to recall how until comparatively recently I still regarded sandwiches with suspicion and scorn.*

*It stemmed from my childhood experience of them. Sandwiches, monotonous mounds as high as the Welsh mountains surrounding my home, were what you were forced to plough through at tea time before being allowed to sink your sweet tooth into the true seduction of the tongue. The jelly, the trifle, the ice-cream, the tinned peaches, the pineapple chunks, the jam tarts, the chocolate cake, the iced sponge. And just about anything fruity encased in my mother's special snowflake-light pastry, submerged in a sunshine pool of piping hot Bird's Custard (my favourite form of refuelling).*

*Tea time is the meal that I remember most vividly from my early years. Especially, somehow, Sunday tea time, when more often than not the chapel preacher would partake with us prior to pounding his evening pulpit. My sullen intake of the obligatory sandwiches, scraped with the inevitable Shippams Fish Paste or ubiquitous home-made damson jam, never failed to cause comment of a moralistic nature. It was pointed out to me by the preacher, revving up for his imminent hell-fire sermon, that the tea-table represented Life itself, if not, indeed, the life of our dear Saviour, Jesus Christ. He, too, had been put upon to endure mortification of the flesh, and solicitude of the soul, before being allowed the enjoyments of the Kingdom of Heaven.*

*I pondered on the miracle of the loaves and fishes, with which Jesus Christ had managed to feed the masses and which no doubt he had to force down himself, in order to keep heart and soul together. How much more harmonious to have summoned up hunks of fruit cake (with whole cherries in) beside the shores of Galilee. But no, boring bread and fish was what he'd chosen. A primitive form of the Bloater Paste between thinly sliced Hovis, which I was mulishly masticating on myself. So who was I, a mere mortal child, to complain? If I did my sacrificial stint now, accommodating all that was dreary and dutiful in my days (sandwiches being somewhere around the top of the list), then the years ahead could be savoured as hedonistic plain sailing. As an adult I'd never eat another sandwich.*

*It didn't work out like that, a complete turn around occurred in my adolescence. When I was fourteen we moved from the warmth of the Welsh womb to the worldly sophistication of a small sweetshop in a London suburb. Business was brisk, sweets were no longer on wartime ration. Both my mother and father slaved full-time in the shop, with my sister and me manning the counter the minute we got home from school, so that our poor parents could snatch a bite to eat. Structured meal times became a social thing of the past. Meat-and-two-veg, followed by a proper pudding, was what my father mourned most and made it plain to us, his womenfolk. But his beseechings reached deaf ears. My mother, the super-cook, had chosen to abandon her culinary calling in favour of the exhilarating ping of the cash till. The jingle of loose change in the pocket of a customer presented more of a challenge than making a perfect apple charlotte. And as for my sister and me – well, what could be a more marvellous meal than a plate piled with Mars Bars, Soft Centres, Coconut Ice and such . . .*

*Within a year I was wanging the weighing scale at over ten stone and crunching aspirins like Smarties for twenty-four hours of the day, to alleviate my excrutiating toothache. My sister fared worse than me, though being older one might have thought she would have been wiser. She lost every single molar in her mouth. The size of an elephant and doomed to dentures at the age of eighteen! We offered to start making real meals for our father.*

*The sandwich was my idea so I accepted the blame, heaped as it was on my head anyway. But it had seemed such a good idea, when I'd seen the illustration for the club sandwich in 'Woman' magazine. A whole meal in itself, that's what it said, to delight the man in your life. More than that, it took barely more than mere minutes to make, once you had the ingredients. Big bread roll from the baker to the right of us, crusty and fresh with a pillow-soft centre. York ham off the bone from the butcher to the left of us. With all the fat removed first because my father followed the feeding habits of Jack Sprat. Lettuce, cucumber, tomatoes, spring onions, beetroot from the greengrocer across the road. And the snazzy touch, a jar of Salad Cream, in place of the suggested mayonnaise in the magazine. Real mayonnaise, certainly the thought of* ***making*** *it myself (!), eluded me until many years later.*

*'Bet he goes berserk!' my sister viewed my club sandwich on completion with less confidence than my triumph deserved. I stood back to survey my small sculpture, piled as high as the mug of steaming tea beside it. There was a surrealist quality to it that engaged me immensely. A sense of fun, of it not being made of anything as mundane as food, and yet it was edible. It had a purpose, it had earned its place in the world. Admittedly, it bore scant resemblance to the club sandwich illustrated, but that had been my fault for putting in the beetroot, not one of the listed fillings. My reason for including it had been purely for the colour (keen on crimson that summer, wearing it top-to-toe). Colour was certainly what my club sandwich was covered in, a virulent pink, from the beetroot having bled into the salad cream and all over everything else.*

*'Well, it's not poison,' I said confidently. 'And I happen to like it. I think my club sandwich is a cheerful sort of chap, seems a shame to think of it being eaten.'*

*'Shouldn't count on that.' My sister could sometimes be spiteful. 'He'll be expecting a proper meal, like sausage-and-mash, and gravy. That I'm good at. Not like yours, where it always goes lumpy.'*

*My father's entry for his food forbade further debate. His outraged disappointment at the tempting fare that I'd proudly placed before him indicated a pressing need for my nifty departure from the room. It wasn't, as my mother later explained to me, that there was anything actually wrong with the meal. Expect that it just wasn't a* ***meal****.*

*'But, everything was in it,' I persisted. Stubborn. Resentful.*

*'Everything.' She agreed, motherly and wise. 'But what you have to understand about men is that they want to see just what they're eating. If you had arranged it all as a salad there wouldn't have been all this fuss, and it would have looked as if you had taken much more time and trouble. Men appreciate that. You'll understand when you're married. It isn't good enough to give your husband a sandwich after he's done a hard day's work. That's what we call the sluttish wife's way.'*

*I got married. More than once. I became something of a hostess of repute, entertaining dinner guests to the tune of twenty, or more, at a time. I shopped and prepared, I cooked and baked, I slaved at the stove (barefoot and pregnant as wives were meant to be then), singing happily, though out of tune, as I did so. I regarded it all as a satisfying labour of love. I didn't offer, or eat, a single sandwich. Ever.*

*And then one day a dazzling pal of mine happened to drop in for a gossip. So caught up were we with the enthralling minutiae of her love life, examining how it was that five-foot-high David (with the equipment of a Dinky Toy) could bring her to orgasm (and so many times!), when the Adonis of her office left her floundering like a goldfish at the bottom of an empty bowl . . . that we completely forgot about lunch.*

*'Oh, a sandwich will do me.' She re-outlined the lush lips, famed for enflaming the length of Fleet Street. 'Got any bacon? Bacon sandwich is what I like eating best in the world – failing a handy supply of the other!'*

*She made the bacon sandwich, a revelation to me. I thought that I had never tasted anything as succulent. And more important than that, I had never before hit upon anything so instant, so immediately satisfying to our needs of that moment. My attitude to sandwiches imperceptively shifted.*

*Involved as I was in those years with my role of Earth Mother to any arty waif and stray with emotional needs and an empty belly, I found most of my reading interests centred on cookery books. The female novelist I preferred was the French writer Colette, purely because of her preoccupation with food. And love. It seemed to be that her characters were always either fornicating or filling their sophisticated faces, the females fascinating their ardent admirers with offerings of 'foie gras' and other such Gallic gastronomic temptations. Nothing simple, like good old baked beans on toast and a cuppa. Nothing speedy, oh no. Even a 'tasse de chocolat' for the youthful sex symbol, Cheri, was prepared by his middle-aged mistress with as much passion and care as she presumably brought to the act of coition itself. Myself, I preferred the earthier approach.*

*Yet still I remain dismissive towards straightforward sandwiches. We had moved from London to the Cornish coast, my second husband and myself, and balmy days were spent on the beach accommodating the gargantuan teenage appetites of our combined brood of sons and daughters. Other parents made picnics easy on themselves with loaves of ready-sliced Mother's Pride, spread with mashed banana or cheese and onion. Simple to pack and transport and distribute. Easy, above all, to eat in high winds and typically British seaside sandstorms. Too easy for me, though, and therefore not allowable. My picnics were a self-imposed nightmare of foil-wrapped flans and quiches, of hardboiled eggs, of home-made pâtés, of cooked chicken legs and breasts, and wholesome bread which had been baked by my own fair hand. Of course! Sumptuous Sunday colour supplement stuff. My mother would have approved of my industry and effort. Ten out of ten for trying. And, more important, for having been seen to have tried.*

*Then all that changed. The children grew up. And we winged off, my spouse and I, to live for a year in the States. 'You do understand, don't you,' he said to me sternly, 'that this slaving of yours over the hot stove has come to an end.' He issued that statement as a command, whilst believing quite genuinely that I would welcome it. See it as some sort of release from a martyred drudgery, not understanding that the cooking belonged to the kitchen side of my character. Just as much as the sexuality belonged to the bedroom bit, or the conversational me demanded a communal drawing-room. In one fell blow I was losing a cosily integrated part of my identity, of my background, of everything that I'd been brought up to believe about food and the preparation of food for loved ones.*

*'What are you saying?' I was desolate. 'That just because there's no family to cook for any more, you're no longer interested in my food?'*

*'I never was very much. I'd sooner see you at the typewriter. I'm just as happy with a sandwich.'*

*We chose to live in a hotel, the legendary Chelsea Hotel, that bastion of raffish, Bohemian eccentrics. Along with our fellow residents – rock stars, writers, Hollywood dissidents, ritzy thespians, penniless painters, ageless persons of immense promise, and others whose lives were exceptional for their total futility – we up-ended the twenty-four hours of each day to suit ourselves and our chosen pursuits. For the second time in my life structured meal times became secondary. The only cooking I did was boiling the electric kettle for instant coffee or tea-bag-in-the-cup tea. But we were in the middle of Manhattan, the fairyland of Fast Food, and I took to it like an exotic fish to tropical waters. Yeah man!*

*There's no doubt about it, that twelve-month in New York sure made its mark on me! My second marriage ended within a mere week of our return to Britain. But the despair (and anyone who denies the despair of divorce is dishonest to themselves and to everyone concerned) was definitely different to the end of my first marriage. Then I'd small children still to cater for. The domestic routine had been structured around family meals. The empty chair at the top of the table served as a searing reminder that things were no longer as they were and never would be again. By the second time around, for me as a single female entity, all that had long since flown out of the window.*

*In the States I had discovered the sandwich. I could claim now that it had affected my whole philosophy or that it echoes my attitudes. Or, more succinctly, my introduction to the American way with sandwiches served to reinforce my feelings about how I'd best like to live my life. That it should be fun and informal, no rules or rigidity. Everything hurled in together, however unexpected or unlikely the ingredients, simply allowing the outcome its own short-lived existence. Tasty moments of pleasure, not judged in terms of soaring success or of crushing defeat. Fellow sandwich addicts understand, as opposed to three-course gourmandisers, that ours is an attitude essentially lacking pretension. The sandwich typifies our disregard, indeed distrust, of anything smacking of high-flown ambition. Our goals are achieved because we limit our aims to what we can just about encompass. We are not interested in failure, our own failure, meaning to say. Nor are we drawn to, and rarely experience, frustration. I have met many a thwarted haute cuisine chef, never a saddened sandwich-maker.*

*The first sandwich to delight my palate, on settling in the States, was called a Reuben. I'd chosen it for its name, which happened to be my father's (out of the Bible – Baptist family). It transported me to seventh heaven, would have taken me even higher had such a place existed. It came in three layers of Russian rye bread grilled until browned, fastened with wooden picks and cut diagonally into thirds. And garnished with glorious French fried potatoes. The squidgy filling was a lathering of Thousand Island dressing, slices of Swiss cheese, splatterings of sauerkraut and alternate layers of corned beef. Mmm, the memory!*

*I have since discovered that the Reuben, regarded now as the sausage-and-mash of the American sandwich scene, was the first champion in the launching of the American National Sandwich Idea Contest, back in*

*1956. This is the granddaddy of all recipe contests over there. Each year, thousands of cooks, chefs, managers, dieticians, waitresses, stewards, students and others in the 'hospitality industry' submit entries to be judged by recognized authorities in the mass-feeding field. Educators from schools of hotel, restaurant and institutional administration, and food editors of newspapers, magazines and trade publications select twenty out of thousands. From these are chosen just four finalists and one of them is the champion. Oh, yes, the sandwich is certainly serious stuff in the States!*

*And who could resist the names they're given? From the Reuben I graduated to sampling all these, amongst others (you can do a hell of a lot of sampling in a twelve-month stay). The Artburger Olivetti – quartered artichoke halves, sliced ripe olives and chopped onions sautéed in melted butter with Worcestershire sauce, lemon juice and garlic butter. All ready to smother over grilled minced beef patties, sandwiched between a split, toasted hamburger bun. Garnished with crisp lettuce leaves, a hefty wedge of lemon and a handful of ripe olives.*

*Tickle the imagination? What would you think these would be? The Snicklefritz. Hank's Pennies of Heaven. Oriental Ladybird. Matador Delite à Go-Go. Private Secretary. Glamorous Clamorous. Plato's Special. Just Ginger Peachy. Hollywood. And Dickens of a Cheese Beef Sandwich. Well, that one is pretty self-explanatory, I suppose. The rest of them you'd have to taste, I can't even remember myself. But the names still stick in my mind.*

*To say that I missed Fast Food when I returned from the States would be the grossest of understatements. The being able to pop down to the corner deli, or just give them a ring and have any of the above delivered to your door. The strolling through Greenwich Village munching peanut butter with crushed pineapple and cranberry relish on rye (bread). Or a slab of white loaf spread with cream cheese and sliced bananas, chopped maraschino cherries, nuts and honey. That's the thing about sandwiches – you just need your hands. No table, no plate, no knife and fork. No nasty washing-up, surely the nicest part of all! It revolutionizes entertaining at home, it really does! I look back on all those dinner parties I gave and I shudder at the thought of starters, middles and afters. I laugh at the thought of meat-and-two-veg, and weep when I consider my wasted sandwich years.*

*It may be the fact of having turned vegetarian that has something to do with it, but I no longer like sitting down to long meals as I used to. The mystique of the right wines with each course has lost its meaning. I'd sooner have a can of lager and a scrumptious sandwich. If the lighting is right (and the companion, of course!) it's just as seductive. The vigorous exchange of ideas with chums can still be as challenging, sprawled each in an easy chair or all over the floor (sticky fingers easily solved with a basket of bright tissues). The sandwich is so easy, so instant, it suits every occasion. It's classless but it fits into every imaginable category. Which is what my pal, Topsy, and I have tried to show in this book – which is why we decided to write it in the first place, I suppose.*

*They say that the newcomer to any scene is the most unfailingly enthusiastic. That the more recent the convert to any cause the more zealous he or she is in spreading the word. Topsy is the culinary expert of the two of us, but an expert with that extra ingredient of imagination that transforms all her offerings into indefinable ambrosia. Hers are the only sandwiches that I've consumed with childish and shameless greed since leaving the States that can compete with any one of the winners that I wolfed down over there. There can be no higher praise than that, not from me. The self-confessed, salivating sandwich-addict.*

*Since I'd chosen to turn out 'A Bit Between the Teeth' with my chum Topsy (she thought of the great title, not me – slightly sickened by that!), it seemed logical and felt right to photograph pals sampling our offerings. We could have gone in for mundane close-ups of selected sandwiches, the same sort of thing that you see in every other sort of recipe book. But that didn't strike me as much fun; this after all is hardly a catalogue of cooked food, not a directive for those in the pursuit of any perfection. Topsy's sandwiches are highly decorative, a delight to the eye, but the true essence of them lies in their edibility. Better to show them being eaten (which I assure you they were within seconds of being snapped!).*

*My long-time colleague, p'raps I should say long-suffering, long-time colleague, Johnny Timbers, was persuaded into taking these most informal of portraits. We remain the closest of friends despite the experience. Food, like babies and boa constrictors, has a mind of its own when it comes to posing for photographs. Could any of us, for instance, have foretold the pathological shyness of lettuce leaves. How even the crispest unfailingly curl up and die once within the range of the wide-angle lens. Of how maddeningly exhibitionist whipped cream can be, running hither and thither under hot studio lights (you should have seen* ***the state*** *of my clothes at the end of the cover snap!).*

*Never mind, we had a good time, and I think that does come across. So take 'A Bit Between the Teeth' and dip in at the deep end. We all invite you most cordially to share our sandwich spread . . . .*

# Bread by Topsy

*Bread, of course, is the basis of any sandwich. Nowadays, the market is full of the most wonderful breads of all shapes and sizes, textures and flavours. Remember, too, that bread on its own is not fattening; it is the filling that determines the number of calories you are consuming.*

*Bread-making must surely be one of the most pleasurable and satisfying means of cooking that there is and it is something that you have literally produced with your own bare hands, kneading and pounding the dough. Then follows the marvellous smell of bread baking in the oven. And what could be better when you have a house full of unexpected guests and no shops open than to bake your own bread. In the following pages you will find a selection of simple recipes to start you off!*

## YEAST

*This is the ingredient that makes bread rise. You can buy it either fresh or dried and both work well. Personally, I prefer using fresh yeast. Both fresh and dried yeast should be stored properly in a cool place. Remember also that the more fat and sugar a dough contains, the more yeast you are going to need.*

***Fresh yeast:*** *This can be bought in most health food shops, some bakers and larger supermarkets. Fresh yeast will keep for up to one week in a screwtop jar or sealed polythene bag in the refrigerator. Don't try freezing it as this takes away its potency.*

***Dried active baking yeast:*** *This is much easier to obtain than fresh yeast and can be found in most supermarkets and health food shops. There are two sorts of dried yeast now available on the market. The first sort has been available for a long time and comes as small, grey granules in either tins or packets. This sort of dried yeast needs reconstitution with sugar and liquid, the amounts varying according to the recipe. The second sort of yeast now available has only been developed recently and can be mixed directly into the flour without having to be reconstituted with sugar and liquid. This yeast looks like fine sand and comes in foil sachets. Dried yeast is twice as concentrated as fresh yeast so you will only need to use half the quantity.*

*You can convert the different yeasts as follows:*

*25 g/1 oz fresh yeast or 1 sachet of easy blend dried yeast. This amount is enough for 675 g/1 ½ lb strong plain flour. When using dried yeast always read the instructions carefully. Dried yeast will keep unopened for about six months. When opened, tins or packets should be kept, tightly sealed, in a cool, dry place.*

## BREADS

***Brown or wheatmeal bread:*** *There are many, many different types of brown bread on the market and many have added wheatgerm or malted meal. The popular brands are usually made from branded flours, and are sold wrapped or sliced for convenience. These are very useful for the sandwich-maker who is in a hurry. They can be bought in thin, medium and thick slices.*

***Wholemeal loaves:*** *Like the brown or wheatmeal breads this variety can be bought almost anywhere. These loaves are coarser than brown or wheatmeal ones and contain important fibres and nutrients essential to our bodies.*

***Germ breads:*** *These breads are baked from white or wheatmeal flours with added wheatgerm, Hovis being about the best-known variety.*

**Bran loaves:** *These are made from either brown or white flour or wholemeal flour with added bran. Nowadays, more people are conscious of the need to eat more bran in their diet for health and vitality. Bran makes bread high in fibre content and gives a very pleasing light texture.*

**Granary breads:** *This bread has a high fibre content and is made from specially formulated flour which is mixed with kibbled and whole grains. These loaves are normally bought unsliced and unwrapped, in both tin and cob varieties. The tin variety is best for sandwich-making because of its shape.*

**Soda loaves:** *These loaves are eaten a great deal in Ireland. They are baked with either brown or white flour and are cooked with bicarbonate of soda or buttermilk instead of yeast.*

**Barrel loaves:** *This is an interesting shape to use for sandwich-making as it has a number of close ridges all the way across the crust which makes it easy to cut. It is also known by other names in different parts of the country, such as lodger's loaf, landlady's loaf or crinkled musket.*

**Bloomer loaves:** *These are long, plumpish loaves, baton-shaped and have deep, diagonal slashes across the top. They are sometimes known also as twists.*

**Batch loaves:** *As the name suggests, these loaves are baked in batches, close together in the oven in one wide tin so that their sides touch. When they are cooked they are then split apart so that they have no side crusts.*

**Crusty baton loaves:** *This is a long, thick, baton-shaped loaf, much thicker and wider than a French stick. It usually has two slashes across the top crust.*

**French stick:** *This is a long, thin loaf with blunt ends and a crusty top. It has long slashes down the centre.*

**Sandwich loaves:** *These are most commonly used for sandwich-making, as the name suggests, as they give even, square slices. They can be bought in either brown or white, in thin, medium or thick slices, ready-wrapped or unsliced and sold under many brand names. They are large, standard loaves, baked in a tin.*

**Split tin loaves:** *These are usually white, long and thin with a slash from end to end along the top of the crust.*

**Baps and rolls:** *These can be made from the same ingredients as used for bread-making but made on a smaller scale. Baps and rolls are often easier to handle than large loaves for sandwich-making as they are easier to fill and to pack. You can use almost any type of filling including hot ones. Baps always take me back to distant days in the Highlands of Scotland, when I had a score of hungry young mouths to feed. Breakfast consisted of steaming bowls of coarse porridge, followed by crispy bacon in large, soft, floury baps and, of course, a good, strong cup of tea.*

**Rye bread:** *This is very good for sandwich-making with its rich, dark colour. It makes a pleasant contrast with colourful ingredients and is a boon for the diet-conscious. Rye bread is made with a mixture of rye and wheat flours and often has a slightly sour taste about it, which, in fact, makes it a rather delicate and unusual-tasting bread. It is particularly good when eaten with smoked fish, cheeses and salads. Rye bread keeps well and can be used when it is quite stale as it still retains its moisture. It should be cut into wafer-thin slices and can be used also to make canapés because of its cutting quality. Rye bread also freezes beautifully.*

***Pitta bread:*** *This bread originally came from the eastern Mediterranean and has become very popular in this country in recent years. It can be bought in most supermarkets, either fresh or frozen. It can take almost any filling and makes a good, robust snack if filled with such things as hamburger, sausages, beans, bacon and eggs, coleslaw and mixed salads. The combinations are endless. Pitta bread packs easily so take it in your hampers for picnics. It is best eaten hot, either toasted or grilled, as it tends to be rather chewy otherwise.*

## *STORING BREAD*

*Ideally, bread should be stored in its original wrapping or in a loosely tied polythene bag. Bread should be kept in a clean, dry container which ensures a good circulation of air. Do not put it in the refrigerator. If you do, this only hastens the process of becoming stale. Keep bread away from strong-smelling foods such as onions and fish, as it becomes tainted.*

*Bread freezes extremely well and it is always useful to have a few different types of bread and rolls in the freezer in case of an emergency. Seal all breads securely in foil or polythene bags, excluding as much air as possible. Label everything clearly. You can freeze uncut loaves for up to two months and rolls and crusty loaves for up to two weeks.*

*Keep bread in its wrappings and thaw at room temperature. Some of the larger loaves may take about four hours to thaw, whereas smaller rolls and breads may only take one hour. If you are in a hurry, bread can be thawed in a moderate oven but will become stale very quickly afterwards. There is no need to thaw sliced bread as it can be toasted from frozen.*

## *BREAD RECIPES*

### *Fast Bread*

25 g/1 oz fresh yeast or
1 sachet easy blend dried yeast
425 ml/¾ pint warm water
1 25-mg ascorbic acid tablet, crushed
675 g/1 ½ lb strong plain flour
1 tablespoonful salt
1 teaspoonful granulated sugar
15 g/½ oz butter or margarine

*Use one 900-g/2-lb tin or two 450-g/1-lb tins. You can minimize the baking time in bread-making considerably by adding ascorbic acid (Vitamin C) to the yeast as they marry well and speed up fermentation.*

*If using fresh yeast, crumble it in the warm water and add the ascorbic acid. Mix the flour, salt and sugar in a separate bowl and rub in the butter or margarine. Make a hole in the middle and pour in the yeast mixture. Mix into a dough. If using easy blend dried yeast, mix it with the flour, sugar and salt. Rub in the butter or margarine. Add the warm water and crushed ascorbic acid tablet and mix to a dough. Knead well for 5-10 minutes. Cover the bowl with clingfilm and leave in a warm place for 5 minutes until the dough has risen by about one-third. Knead again lightly. Mould the dough into the shape of the tin and put into one larger or two smaller tins. Cover completely with clingfilm and leave in a warm place for about 30-40 minutes until the dough has risen to twice the size. Bake in a preheated hot oven, 220°C, 425°F, Gas Mark 7, for 30-35 minutes. Cool on a wire rack.*

### *Instant breakfast rolls*

4 heaped tablespoonfuls self-raising flour
Generous pinch of salt
Milk or milk and water mixed

*Put the flour into a bowl and add the salt. Mix the flour to a fairly stiff dough with milk or milk and water. If you have no milk you can use just water on its own. Shape the dough into rolls and place them, spaced out, on a floured baking tray. Make a cross on top of each roll and put in a preheated hot oven, 220°C, 425°F, Gas Mark 7 and bake for 15-20 minutes or until they are to your liking. Eat them hot with lashings of butter or fill them with crispy bacon, eggs, sausages or whatever else you like.*

### *Scotch Baps*

225 g/8 oz strong plain flour
1 level teaspoonful salt
15 g/½ oz fresh yeast or
½ sachet easy blend dried yeast
150 ml/¼ pint warm milk
150 ml/¼ pint warm water
25 g/1 oz butter

*If using fresh yeast, mix together the milk and water and dissolve the yeast in it. Sift the flour and salt together in a large bowl, rub the butter into the flour and stir in the yeast mixture. If using easy blend dried yeast, mix together the flour, yeast and salt and rub in the butter. Add the milk and water mixed together.*

*Mix to a rough dough in the bowl, then turn it out and knead until smooth. Put the dough back into the bowl and cover with a large polythene bag. Leave to rise for about 1 hour in a warm place until twice its size.*

*When the dough has risen, turn it out onto a board and press it out with your knuckles to knock out any air. Divide the dough into six portions and roll into a ball with your hands. Then, using a rolling pin, flatten each roll slightly to make a round bap. Place onto a greased baking tray and brush with milk. Dust with flour and leave in a warm place for about 15 minutes until risen and fluffy.*

*Just before baking, dust the baps again with flour and press a floured thumb into the centre of each bap. Place in a preheated hot oven, 220°C, 425°F, Gas Mark 7 and bake for 15-20 minutes. The baps are best served freshly baked, when slightly hot. They can also be heated up by placing in a warm oven for about 5 minutes.*

### *Herby Bread*

150 ml/¼ pint milk
150 ml/¼ pint warm water
15 g/½ oz fresh yeast or
½ sachet easy blend dried yeast
275 g/10 oz wholewheat flour
4 teaspoonfuls granulated sugar
1 teaspoonful salt
25 g/1 oz butter
1 small onion, peeled and grated
½ teaspoonful dried rosemary
½ teaspoonful dried oregano
Pinch of freshly grated nutmeg
1-2 teaspoonfuls aniseed

*You need a 450-g/1-lb loaf tin. If using fresh yeast mix together the milk and water. Blend in the fresh yeast. Combine the flour, sugar and salt in a large bowl and rub in the butter. Add the onion, rosemary, oregano and nutmeg and pour in the yeast mixture. If using easy blend dried yeast, mix together the flour, yeast, sugar and salt and rub in the butter. Add the onion, rosemary, oregano and nutmeg. Add the milk and water mixed together. Mix together to make a dough and knead for 10-15 minutes. Put the dough in a mixing bowl, cover with clingfilm and leave in a warm place until the dough has doubled in size. This should take about 45 minutes.*

*Knead the dough again lightly and mould it into the shape of the tin. Sprinkle with aniseed and place into the greased loaf tin. Cover and leave to rise in a warm place for about ½ hour. Bake in a preheated hot oven, 200°C, 400°F, Gas Mark 6, for about 25 minutes. Serve the bread hot.*

***Granary Cob***

25 g/1 oz fresh yeast or
1 sachet easy blend dried yeast
425 ml/¾ pint warm water
675 g/1½ lb granary flour
1 tablespoonful salt
1 tablespoonful granulated sugar
25 g/1 oz butter
Cracked wheat for topping

*For anyone with a large appetite, this loaf is delicious split open and filled with a variety of things such as sausages, eggs, bacon, salads and fish. This recipe will make a 900 g/2 lb loaf.*

*If using fresh yeast, dissolve it in a small amount of the warm water in a small bowl or cup. Put the flour, salt and sugar into a large bowl and rub in the butter. Pour in the yeast mixture, add the remaining warm water and mix into a dough. If using easy blend dried yeast mix the flour, yeast, salt and sugar together and rub in the butter. Add the warm water and mix to a dough. Knead well for 5-10 minutes, return the dough to the bowl and cover with clingfilm. Set aside in a warm place until the dough has doubled in size (this should take about 1 hour). Knead the dough lightly and shape it into a round. Sprinkle it with cracked wheat.*

*Place the dough onto a greased baking sheet and cut a deep cross on the top. Cover and leave in a warm place until well risen. Place in a preheated hot oven, 220°C, 425°F, Gas Mark 7, and bake for 40-45 minutes.*

***Pitta Bread***

15 g/½ oz fresh yeast or
½ sachet easy blend dried yeast
275 ml/½ pint warm water
450 g/1 lb wholewheat flour
2 teaspoonfuls salt
1 teaspoonful granulated sugar
1 tablespoonful olive oil

*If using fresh yeast, crumble into a bowl and mix with the water until dissolved. In a separate bowl combine the flour, salt, sugar and oil, add the yeast mixture and mix well to a dough. If using easy blend dried yeast, mix with the flour, salt and sugar. Add the water and oil and mix to a dough. Knead well for 5 minutes.*

*Cover the dough with clingfilm and leave in a warm place for about 1 hour until the dough has doubled in bulk. Remove the clingfilm and knead the dough again for about 2 minutes. Divide into 12 equal pieces and roll each piece out into an oval, flattened shape. Place onto a greased baking sheet, well apart. Put the sheet in a warm place for about 15 minutes until the pieces of dough are larger and puffy. Place them in a preheated hot oven, 220°C, 425°F, Gas Mark 7, for about 5 minutes and then reduce the heat to 200°C, 400°F, Gas Mark 6, for 10 minutes. Remove from the oven and cool on a wire rack.*

## *SOME USEFUL TIPS*

*I freely admit that most of these hints are no more than normal common sense. But I include them with no apology and no sense whatsoever of 'talking down'. They are passed on in the hope of steering you past pitfalls into which I myself have fallen; pitfalls which, at the least, are infuriating and which, at worst, necessitate a last-minute dash to the shops, usually when time is already running tight.*

*The sort of problem which I am attempting to anticipate and to guide you through is not that which confronts the housewife who is knocking up a simple sandwich snack for husband and children; hasty improvisation can normally provide an adequate solution in such circumstances. Rather than that, I have in mind the occasion for which you have planned courses of sandwiches carefully chosen to complement one another – rather in the same way that a formal four-course dinner needs careful construction – and which leaves little room for last-minute adjustment.*

## *BUYING*

*One of my cardinal rules is always to buy everything in quantities somewhat in excess of my actual anticipated needs. This may sound extravagant, but effectively it never seems to result in total wastage. Whatever is left over always comes in handy for something – even if only to liven up my Shi-Tzu's tin of 'Doggy Din'.*

*Bread is one area where I am especially careful to allow for more than I think I shall need, whether I am buying or baking my own. The reason for this is that all too often loaves develop holes when rising in the oven, and holey slices of bread are the very opposite of God's gift to sandwich-makers.*

*Most large, ready-cut loaves contain twenty-two slices – not counting the heels – or enough for eleven sandwiches. So it's a fairly simple exercise in mathematics to decide how many loaves you will need for your quantity of sandwiches. Having arrived at the answer, buy at least one more – or, in the case of large numbers, two or even three more, the same principle applying if you are baking your own.*

*A great many of my recipes include salads. It's impossible to say how far a lettuce will stretch because they vary so hugely in size and body. The same with cucumbers; they come in all lengths, so follow my advice and buy more than you think you will need. Lettuces keep well for a day or two in the salad drawer of the refrigerator. If you carve a cross into the stalk of a cucumber and stand it in a jar with an inch or two of fresh water, it should remain fresh and crisp for several days.*

*The average supermarket tomato will probably yield no more than four slices or five at the very most – if, like me, you discard the two end cuts. I allow three slices for each sandwich and even now I am still surprised at the quantity of tomatoes which I have to buy for the salad content of a batch of sandwiches. But don't worry if you find you have bought more than you actually use; tomatoes, too, keep perfectly in the salad compartment of the refrigerator.*

*As for the rest of the complementary additives to your sandwiches, the same rule-of-thumb applies: buy large jars of chutneys, mayonnaise, mustards, ketchups and apple sauce – all will keep perfectly, as will butter and soft margarine spread.*

*It is impossible to be precise about the exact quantity or weight of meat, fish and fowl that you will need for each sandwich. I like to make my sandwiches substantial and perhaps I am more generous with my fillings than most people. Anyway, I will give you the few simple rules which I apply in the hope that they will give you some useful guidelines.*

***Meat:*** *For meat which I buy on the bone, I normally allow 65-75 g/2½-3 oz per sandwich. Meats without a bone – beef, tongue and corned beef – require about 50 g/2 oz for each sandwich. For hamburgers I allow a good 75 g/3 oz of meat.*

***Poultry and game:*** *The average 1.3 kg/2½ lb chicken will stretch to about eight sandwiches if, like me, you use the legs as well as the breast. For turkey fillings I use only the breast and allow up to 50 g/2 oz cooked weight per portion. Incidentally, the legs are never wasted – I devil them or make them into curry. Both are delicious! Pheasant and duck make marvellous fillings, but sadly both are outrageously expensive. The breast of either bird is all that you can use; from a pheasant you will get four good sandwiches, while a duck will yield no more than three. The rest of the duck is good for little other than soup. The remains of the pheasant do much better, however; my trick is to roast the pheasant with stewing steak inside it, which afterwards I cut into chunks along with the leg meat and bake them with plenty of mushrooms in a pie.*

***Fish:*** *I allow about 50 g/2 oz for each filling. Don't throw away the skin and the scraps. Stew them in milk as the basis of a seafood soup. 50 g/2 oz is about right for shelled prawns or shrimps.*

***Cheese:*** *Again the magical measurement of about 50 g/2 oz applies, although very strong Cheddar may require a bit less.*

***Eggs:*** *Last but not least, that good old friend of the sandwich-maker, the humble egg. I always allow one large egg for each filling.*

## *PREPARATION*

*For most of my sandwich fillings my blender is my main weapon of attack, but I don't intend to insult your intelligence by treating you to a lesson on how to put a batch of hardboiled eggs through a blender! But for meat and poultry sandwiches I have devised a few tips which I find handy and perhaps they merit being passed onto you.*

*Let's start with lamb. I always use the shoulder. Not only is it the most economical joint, but for me it just has the edge on the leg in terms of flavour. The disadvantages are that it carries more fat than the leg and it is not so easy to carve. But for sandwiches, the slices don't have to look pretty, and I have developed my own method of carving the shoulder for sandwich fillings. I remove the meat from the top of the shoulder blade by easing a really sharp knife horizontally under the flesh from the corners of the bone towards the 'fin' which runs down its centre. Then I make a firm vertical incision on each side of the 'fin' and draw the flesh away from the bone. I repeat the same process on the underside of the bone, which is easier because it is almost flat and has no 'fin'. Then, take off the skin and cut out all the fat; now the lamb is ready for the slicer. Cut the remainder of the meat away from the bone in rough hunks, and, of course, before it goes through the slicer all the skin and fat are removed.*

*As for pork, I admit without shame that I shop around for the cheapest cut that I can find, and often I have no idea which part I am buying. After roasting the joint –*

*always slowly to ensure even cooking right through to the bone – I cut off all the skin and fat and cut the meat away from the bone in three or four chunks for putting through the slicer.*

*Although it is not the most glamorous of cuts, for beef sandwiches I always buy topside. If you want to jazz it up a bit, marinate it for a few hours in red wine with some mixed herbs and mustard, turning it every so often. Be sure not to over-cook it; beef sandwiches are ruined if the meat is dried up and brown. As with pork and lamb, before feeding it through the slicer I remove the roll of fat and carve the meat into three or four chunky pieces.*

*For chicken fillings, carve all the meat into little slivers and make sure to mix it all well together so that each sandwich gets a fair share of brown and white meat. The breast of the turkey is all that I normally use, and I find that it is a particularly easy beast to carve into wafer-thin slices. Pheasant breasts, too, are easy to carve really thinly. With poultry and game, I remove the skin before carving.*

*Duck is the one exception to this rule. The skin is delicious and I have my own method of carving duck so that each slice has its own bit of skin. I make a firm incision down the length of the breast and then fold the meat away to either side of the carcass, easing the flesh from the bone with a sharp knife.*

*My local delicatessen carves my hams, salamis and other continental sausages really thinly and for salamis and the like they do me a special favour. First, they remove the skin to whatever depth I require. Then they cut down the sausage vertically, so that when it goes through the slicer the end product is a neat pile of semicircular slices. The reason for this exercise is that when making up the sandwiches I place the flat side of the semicircles along the edge of the slice of bread to ensure that the meat fills the sandwich right up to the corners.*

## PREPARING LARGE QUANTITIES

*If you are making large numbers of sandwiches, a few moments of thought and forward planning will make the whole performance less confusing and frustrating and is unquestionably time well spent. My main suggestions are as follows in the sequence which I find most practical.*

*First, prepare all of the ingredients of your fillings, including salad components and the like, and line them up in plastic bowls or freezer containers. Then take out all the jars of mayonnaise, mustard, chutney and so on which you are going to need and remove their lids – there's nothing more frustrating than trying to unscrew an unopened jar of mayonnaise when your fingers are a bit greasy with butter! Then place a knife or other serving implement in each one.*

*Next, butter all the bread, and leaving exactly half of the buttered slices to one side, arrange the remainder of the bread in rows on your work surface. The next move is to divide out the fillings and I have found that there is a right and wrong way to go about even this exercise. If, for example, I am making up six curried chicken sandwiches, I aim to spoon out six splodges which are rather less than one-sixth of the entire mixture. Then I go round again, topping up each one from whatever remains. If this seems like an unnecessary waste of time I do find it much more practical than running out of filling after I have doled out only five spoonfuls and having to steal a bit from each to make up the sixth.*

*Now is the time for adding the mustards and the like – but not the mayonnaise – before you add the salad content. When this step is completed, all that remains is to spread the surface of the second slice with mayonnaise for those sandwiches that require it and then to close the sandwich.*

*The next step is cutting – and perhaps wrapping also – for both of which you will need your cutting-board. I place the knife across the bread corner-wise, but before I begin to cut, I put my free hand on top of the knife across the sandwich so as to hold it firm and to prevent the bread from tearing or the contents from spilling out.*

*I then fold one half on top of the other and put the sandwiches on a plate for meals or parties in the home, or aside for wrapping in clingfilm for outside occasions.*

*Sandwiches prepared in advance can be kept perfectly fresh for three or four hours simply by keeping them well covered. The method I favour is a damp tea towel, well wrung-out and spread over the plate of sandwiches with its sides and corners tucked in under the dish. When the cover is removed, the sandwiches will be fresh and lively and the bread will be neither stale nor soggy.*

## *PACKING*

*For outside occasions I always set my sandwiches on a tray or in a shallow basket, lying on one of their short sides so that their 'faces' are visible. Not only does this make their contents easily recognizable without having to pick them up, turn them and generally maul them about; it also prevents them from getting squashed and tired looking, which is how they will end up if stacked on their sides, layer upon layer in a deep hamper.*

## *BUTTERING*

*If you are using butter as opposed to a soft-butter substitute spread, do try to remember to take it out of the refrigerator some hours beforehand – the length depends on the temperature of your kitchen. If you happen to find yourself caught on the hop and when making-up time arrives your butter is still hard, do avoid the temptation to put the butter in the oven or under the grill. Both methods serve only to turn the outside of the block to oil while the core remains hard as a rock.*

*Instead, pour boiling water into a heatproof jug. Get two or three knives and immerse their blades in the boiling water. Then, using them in rotation, scrape the knives along the top of the block of butter, bringing it up in folds. The heat from the blade should be just sufficient to facilitate spreading.*

*If you are using an uncut loaf – especially if you are preparing dainty 'Tea at the Ritz'-type sandwiches for which the bread needs to be cut wafer thin – always butter straight onto the loaf so that when you cut your slices from the loaf they are already buttered. This method overcomes the problem of the bread tearing when the butter is applied, which can happen all too easily if you try to butter bread which has been sliced really thin.*

*This leads to two further points which I will include here for want of a more appropriate section. Firstly, if you are making very delicate sandwiches, it's a good idea to use bread that is a day old. Secondly, if you want to remove the crusts, be sure to fill your sandwiches before cutting the crusts away from the bread.*

## *SLICING AND CARVING*

*I am fortunate enough to have a meat slicer. If, like me, you regularly make large numbers of sandwiches, especially ones with beef and pork fillings, I would urge you to buy one as it is an investment which pays real dividends.*

*I have already described how I carve my cuts of pork and beef into three or four chunky portions. This done, I feed them through the slicer with one of the smaller sides of the chunk offered to the blade. This method results in small slices of meat – as thin as you want – usually no bigger than a large postage stamp or a match box.*

*My reason for preferring small slices, particularly of beef and of pork, is that both can be chewy and difficult to bite through cleanly. Small slices of meat prevent that wretched fiasco, when at the very first chomp on the sandwich, the entire meat content is dragged out from between the bread, leaving behind two empty slices.*

*For large quantities I use my slicer for lamb, corned beef, salt beef and other meats, which although not as chewy as topside, I prefer to use in small pieces to make the eating more pleasant.*

*Hams (other than Parma hams), salamis and most varieties of Continental sausages and tongue also do not absolutely demand the same treatment; any reasonably serviceable set of teeth should be capable of making a clean job of biting through the sandwich without mishap.*

*If you want to buy a bit of time in advance by doing your roasting the day before or in the morning for an evening party, don't be tempted to carve and slice your meats more than two hours ahead. I find that all meats and poultry lose some of their colour and taste if sliced too far in advance, even if kept cool and in a sealed container. So my advice is to leave the meat whole and on the bone, if there is one, until the last practical moment.*

## *HOT SANDWICHES*

*Many people shy away from the thought of hot sandwiches only because they have not got a toaster. I do own one but seldom use it. The reasons are twofold: I find I get better results using the grill or the oven, and while my toaster makes only two sandwiches at a go, my grill can turn out a batch of four and my oven six. Furthermore, since I like my fillings to be really generous, my sandwiches are just too bulky to squeeze into my toaster. The only drawback to grilled or oven-cooked sandwiches is that they do, of course, need to be turned.*

*This is how I perform this potentially tricky operation: From the shop where I bought my stove I obtained an extra grid for the grill. After arranging four sandwiches on the grid in the grilling tray place the spare grid on top. Then slide the tray under the grill on the lower grilling level, and when the time for turning arrives, remove the tray from under the grill and grip both grids through a good pair of oven gloves. Turn the whole thing over so that the toasted sides are on the underneath. Return the grids to the tray and place under the grill to cook the second sides.*

*For oven-cooked sandwiches arrange them on a flat baking sheet that has no rims. When the top layer of bread is a golden colour remove the baking sheet from the oven and loosen all the sandwiches with a knife. Place a second baking sheet which has been warming in the oven on top of the sandwiches and, gripping both trays firmly, invert them. Remove the original sheet and place the second sheet back in the oven to cook the second sides.*

*For grilling I always have my grill at full blast. For oven-cooked sandwiches preheat the oven to around 180°C, 350°F, Gas Mark 4. The time needed for cooking the sandwiches depends on various things such as which type of bread you are using and the fierceness of the grill you are using. The easy rule is that when the top slices of bread are golden-brown, presto! the time has arrived to turn them over.*

*For all grilled or oven-cooked sandwiches remember the following points:*

**1.** *In order to ensure that the bread comes out crispy and tasty, brush lightly with oil or melted butter on both outsides of the sandwich. Where suitable and to give an added bit of flavour, I sometimes stir a pinch of peeled and crushed garlic into the oil or melted butter.*

**2.** *In my opinion, no salad ingredients – other than tomato – should be included in cooked sandwiches. Also, I tend to use mayonnaise very sparingly if at all.*

**3.** *If you want to have no crusts on your cooked sandwiches remove them after cooking, not beforehand.*

**4.** *Whether grilling or using the oven, always remember to grip the grids or baking sheets firmly when turning the sandwiches to make sure that they don't slide out. Wear an apron and stand back; a fair amount of drips is almost unavoidable and you do not want them to spoil your party dress.*

**5.** *Serve all hot sandwiches immediately while piping hot.*

*There is no particular chapter in this book reserved entirely for grilled or oven-cooked sandwiches. There are suggestions for hot sandwiches in most of the chapters and the index can be used for guidance.*

## OPEN SANDWICHES

*No sandwich book can consider itself really complete without at least a reference to open sandwiches. Indeed, they can be delicious and undoubtedly have plenty of visual appeal. Their main drawback is that they do require a knife and fork as well as a plate. In this book I have kept to sandwiches which positively require no other implements than those with which Nature equipped us – fingers and thumbs and a set of teeth.*

*Open sandwiches do not lend themselves to easy transportation to point to points, open-air theatres and offices. If you are going to serve up open sandwiches to your guests at home, everyone has to be able to sit down and then you might as well serve up a meal of meat and two veg. This said, many of my recipes are obviously suitable to use for making open sandwiches and if this is the type that you favour for any particular occasion, don't let me put you off.*

*Whether they are open or not, the concept of this book is to persuade you that sandwiches – really good ones – can replace the more traditional style of meal, both satisfyingly and excitingly.*

# TOTS AT TEA TIME

*Though I say it myself, I'm a pretty terrific hostess of tots' tea times. I started young at the game, at about five years old in my primary school when I invited the whole class of infants home for tea at my house – on condition that they all brought me a present. No present, no entry. I made that clear from the start, but it didn't put anyone off – they all turned up as commanded, to the sweet astonishment of my sainted mother. 'But it isn't even your birthday!' she bewailed, doling out biscuits and what was left of the Christmas cake. 'Whatever could have possessed you to think of such a thing?' 'When I woke up this morning I felt in the mood for a party and for getting lots of presents, that's all.' So, it is claimed, was my innocent answer; confounding the adults with the signs of an early existentialist attitude to life – or, more cynically, a leaning towards pampered self-indulgence. Extravagance, as long as someone else was doing the work and footing the bill. It was soon enough stamped out of me!*

*But I* ***loved*** *parties as a tot, giving them or going to them. I still do, doesn't everyone deep down inside? And when I still had tiny tots in the house I made sure that each celebration should be one that they'd remember for the rest of their lives. Whether they do or not is another matter, but they remain in my mind – if only for the amount of thought and imagination I had put into them. Though, curiously, the one which was the most successful actually took the least effort of all.*

*It was when I had started in my most exacting job in journalism, not long after my first divorce. Planning the usual complicated catering was out of the question. All I had time for was a rushed purchase of twenty plastic carrier bags with a Mickey Mouse motif, filling each one with junk food, the sort that kids love. Smith's crisps, assorted flavours so that a lot of swapping could take place. Boxes of Smarties. Cans of Coke, lemonade, ginger beer. Bags of nuts and raisins. Bars of chocolate. Liquorice sticks. Apples. Oranges. Bananas. Sweet plums. Peaches. The contents of each bulging bag being identical to the next to avoid accusations of favouritism and consequent quarrels. There were no quarrels, only total and happy abandonment. I'd borrowed a Land-Rover from a country friend and ferried all twenty suitably scruffy tots to the Adventure Playground in Holland Park, having warned all parents first not to send them in satin and lace. Only one boy had a bad time, in disgrace for wetting his pants. Scolded in full view of all the others by his mother, who had insisted on coming along 'to keep an eye on him, and see he behaved himself'. Poor little mite. Over-protected. I wonder how he's turned out, now in his early twenties? Hopefully not still hampered by his mother as chaperone.*

*It's a funny thing about tiny ones and what they like to eat at special tea times. You find them gobbling down things that they wouldn't touch at home, as long as it looks strange and exotic enough. All Topsy's offerings for tots take on a slightly surreal appearance. It must come from having reared five kids herself (four daughters and one son), and knowing just what appeals to their sense of humour. The minute Hovis loaves she uses, for instance, are a particular favourite. The peanut and sardine offering dotted with upright salted peanuts to look just like baby hedgehogs. Those were the ones that vanished fastest when we did our first photo session. I say first photo session because we had to do a second shoot on this, using only one tiny child, Charlie. The first didn't – well, – quite work out . . .*

*'I'd rather not use my own little lads,' Johnny had said that from the start. It was me who'd insisted. 'But William and Tom are so* ***handsome*** *(they're six and three). And we can take them with their little pals, those two called Alice. They are* ***adorable****. (I go soppy about small persons now I haven't any of my own – I'm just longing to be a granny, that's the thing.)*

*When the snaps came through, well, I sort of saw what he meant. 'Photographers should never use their own kids on a professional job,' Johnny says. 'The children don't give the same respect and attention that they would to a stranger, someone who isn't forever snapping them around the house.' Point taken, I stand corrected. And actually after watching even four tots tackling Topsy's tea time fare, I wondered whether all those kiddies' tea parties were* ***really*** *as idyllic as I choose to remember....*

## PEANUT BUTTER

- 2 thin slices of bread
- Butter
- Thick and crunchy peanut butter
- 1 banana, mashed
- ¼ teaspoonful caster sugar

Butter both slices of bread and spread with peanut butter. Mix the mashed banana with the sugar and spread on top of peanut butter. Cover with the second slice of bread.

## PEANUT BUTTER AND PINEAPPLE

- 2 thin slices of bread
- Thick and crunchy peanut butter
- 1 tablespoonful crushed fresh pineapple
- 1 dessertspoonful thick honey

Spread both slices of bread thickly with peanut butter. Mix the crushed pineapple with the honey and heap onto one slice of the bread. Cover with the second slice.

## PEANUT BUTTER AND STRAWBERRY JAM

- 2 thin slices of bread
- Butter
- 1 dessertspoonful peanut butter
- 1 dessertspoonful strawberry jam

Butter both slices of bread. Spread the peanut butter evenly over one slice and then add the strawberry jam. Cover with the second slice of bread and cut into small sandwich portions.

## SARDINE AND EGG

- 2 thin slices of bread
- Butter
- 2 sardines in oil, well drained
- A few drops of lemon juice
- 1 teaspoonful mayonnaise
- ½ hard boiled egg, mashed
- Salt and white pepper
- 2-3 slices wafer-thin cucumber

Butter both slices of bread. Mash the sardines with the lemon juice and spread on one slice of the bread. Mix the mayonnaise, egg, salt and pepper together and spread on top of the sardine mixture. Cover with the slices of cucumber and top with the second slice of bread.

## SAUSAGES, BEANS AND BACON

- 1 rasher streaky bacon
- 2 slices of bread
- Butter
- 1 sausage, cooked and thinly sliced
- 1 dessertspoonful cold baked beans
- ½ small tomato, skinned and thinly sliced
- 1-2 crisp lettuce leaves

Remove the rinds from the bacon, crisply cook and dice it. Butter both slices of bread. Place the sausage, bacon, baked beans and tomato on one slice of bread. Put the lettuce leaves on top. Cover with the second slice of bread. This is also very good toasted.

## BAKED BEANS, EGG AND BACON

- A little butter
- 1 egg, beaten
- A little milk
- Salt and freshly ground black pepper
- 4 rashers of streaky bacon
- 2 medium slices of bread
- Oil or melted butter
- 1 heaped dessertspoonful cold baked beans
- Salt and freshly ground black pepper
- 1 heaped dessertspoonful grated mild Cheddar cheese

Melt the butter in a small non-stick pan, mix in the egg, milk, salt and pepper. Cook gently until the mixture is just firm, remove from the heat and cool. Remove the rinds from the bacon and crisply cook it. Brush one side of both slices of bread with oil or butter. Spread the beans over the dry surface of one slice and arrange the bacon on top. Add the scrambled egg and the seasoning. Cover with the grated cheese. Cover with the second slice of bread, the oiled or buttered side up. Cook in a preheated oven, 200°C, 400°F, Gas Mark 6, or under the grill until golden and crisp.

## HAMBURGER WITH FRANKFURTERS AND COLESLAW

*100 g/¼ lb good minced beef*
*A pinch of mixed herbs*
*¼ teaspoonful tomato ketchup*
*¼ teaspoonful Worcestershire sauce*
*¼ small white cabbage*
*1 carrot*
*¼ onion*
*¼ sweet green pepper*
*1 dessertspoonful mayonnaise*
*Salt and freshly ground black pepper*
*A few drops of lemon juice*
*1 15-cm/6-in piece of French stick*
*Butter*
*1 dessertspoonful tomato ketchup*
*2 Frankfurters, sliced in half lengthways*
*¼ tomato, sliced*
*1-2 crisp lettuce leaves*
*English mustard*

*Mix together the minced beef, herbs, ketchup and Worcestershire sauce. Bind into a flattish, round ball and grill to your taste – rare, medium or well done. Leave to cool.*

*To make the coleslaw slice the cabbage, carrot, onion and green pepper thinly. Mix the vegetables with the mayonnaise, salt, pepper and lemon juice, making sure that the mayonnaise has covered all the ingredients thoroughly. Slice the bread in half and butter each slice. Spread the ketchup on one slice and cover with the hamburger, coleslaw, Frankfurters, tomato and lettuce. Spread the second slice with mustard and cover the sandwich. This is also very good toasted, but remember to lightly toast the inside of the bread before filling to prevent the bread from becoming too mushy.*

## TONGUE AND EGG SALAD

*2 slices of bread or 1 roll*
*Butter*
*1-2 slices of cooked lamb's tongue*
*1 hardboiled egg, mashed*
*Mayonnaise*
*Salt and freshly ground black pepper*
*1-2 slices of mature Cheddar cheese*
*¼ tomato, sliced*
*1-2 sprigs of watercress*
*1-2 crisp lettuce leaves*
*Mustard*
*Mayonnaise*

*Butter both slices of bread or halves of roll. Place the tongue on one slice or half of roll. Mash the egg with the mayonnaise and season to taste. Spread this mixture onto the tongue and top with the cheese, tomato, watercress and lettuce. Spread the second slice of bread or roll with mustard and mayonnaise and cover the sandwich.*

## CREAMED CHICKEN AND HAM

- 2 medium slices of bread
- Butter
- 25 g/1 oz mixture of cooked chicken and ham
- 1 dessertspoonful mayonnaise
- Dash of Worcestershire sauce
- Salt and freshly ground black pepper
- 1-2 crisp lettuce leaves

Butter both slices of bread. Mince the chicken and ham together. Mix the minced chicken and ham with the mayonnaise and Worcestershire sauce and season to taste. Heap the mixture onto one slice of the bread and top with the lettuce leaves. Cover with the second slice of bread.

## SCRAMBLED EGG AND MARMITE

- A little butter
- 1 egg, beaten
- A little milk
- Salt and freshly ground black pepper
- 2 thin slices of bread
- Marmite
- 1 tomato, skinned and thinly sliced

Melt the butter in a small non-stick pan, mix in the egg, milk, salt and pepper. Cook gently until the mixture is just firm, remove from the heat and cool. Spread marmite on one slice of bread and cover with the scrambled egg. Top with the tomato and cover with the second slice of bread. Cut into quarters.

## CHEESE AND CRACKERS

- ½ tart apple
- ¼ mandarin orange
- 2 cream crackers
- Butter
- 1 tablespoonful cream cheese
- 1 teaspoonful raisins

Thinly slice and core the apple but do not peel. Peel the orange and remove the pith and pips. Spread the cream crackers with butter. Spread the cream cheese on one cracker and top with the apple, mandarin and raisins. Top with the second cracker.

## CHOCOLATE SURPRISE

*2 medium slices of bread*
*Butter*
*1 teaspoonful cream cheese*
*1 teaspoonful clear honey*
*½ chocolate flake*
*1 teaspoonful salted peanuts*

Butter both slices of bread. Mash the cream cheese with the honey and spread the mixture on one slice of bread. Crumble the chocolate flake on top and add the peanuts. Cover with the second slice of bread.

## CHOCOLATE SPREAD WITH GROUND ALMONDS

*2 thin slices of bread*
*Butter*
*1 dessertspoonful ground almonds*
*1 tablespoonful chocolate spread*

Butter both slices of the bread. Stir the ground almonds into the chocolate spread. Smooth the mixture over one of the slices of bread and top with the second slice. Remove the crusts and slice into small pieces.

## CHOCOLATE, HONEY AND NUTS

*2 thin slices of bread*
*Butter*
*1 dessertspoonful thick honey*
*½ chocolate flake*
*25g/1 oz crushed hazelnuts*

Butter both slices of bread and spread with honey. Crumble the chocolate flake and put it on one slice of bread. Top with the hazelnuts and cover with the second slice of bread.

## RASPBERRY JAM WITH HUNDREDS AND THOUSANDS

*2 thin slices of bread*
*Butter*
*1 dessertspoonful raspberry jam*
*1 teaspoonful hundreds and thousands*

Butter both slices of bread. Spread the jam on one slice of bread and sprinkle with the hundreds and thousands. Cover with the second slice of bread and cut into small portions.

## FRIED BANANA AND BROWN SUGAR

*2 thin slices of bread*
*Butter*
*1 banana*
*Double cream*
*Brown sugar*

*Butter both slices of bread. Split the banana into halves lengthways and fry it gently in a small amount of butter until golden brown and soft. Drain and arrange the halves on one slice of bread. Pour on top a generous helping of whipped double cream. Sprinkle liberally with brown sugar. Cover with the second slice of bread and cut into small portions.*

## BANANA AND MARSHMALLOWS

*2 thin slices of bread*
*Butter*
*1 banana, mashed with lemon juice*
*Hundreds and thousands*
*1-2 marshmallows, roughly sliced*

*Butter both slices of bread. Cover one slice with the mashed banana. Sprinkle generously with hundreds and thousands, top with the marshmallows and cover with the second slice of bread.*

## DATE AND BANANA

*2 medium slices of bread*
*Butter*
*1 banana, mashed*
*1 teaspoonful brown sugar*
*2-3 fresh dates, with stones removed*
*1 dessertspoonful crushed walnuts*

*Butter both slices of bread. Spread the mashed banana on one slice and cover with the sugar, dates and walnuts. Top with the second slice of bread.*

# Hamper for Open-air Theatres

*I'm an **aficionado** of open-air theatre-going. I got into it (as they say) after seeing my first Punch and Judy show on the beach in Porthcawl, slavering all the while on a Wall's wafer. What I liked as much as anything was the doing of two things at once. Being enthralled by performances and eating at the same time. Or drinking. The thing I abhor about the legitimate theatre is that ghastly rush during the interval to gulp down your gin and tonic, and having to keep quiet whilst searching for the coffee soft centre (ending up with the nougat – disaster for dentures!).*

*But it was as an art student in Italy that I graduated to grander things. I'd gone on a travelling scholarship (my father all but killed off the trade in our tobacconist shop, by boasting to customers of my award. So much so that by the end my mother banned him from behind the counter – which was probably what he'd been after all the time.) The trip started off in Verona and ended up in Venice and on the first night I went to the Verona Coliseum to see a performance of 'Aida'. There were real-life elephants on stage and a thousand stars in the sky. At a certain point everyone lit a candle in the audience and that's all you could see, the stage, the stars, and the little candlelights. It was around midnight and I was more moved by the experience than I could have admitted, but there were other things on my mind. I was absolutely famished.*

*It hadn't occurred to me to take anything to eat, but the moment all the surrounding families started spreading feasts on their laps, I saw too keenly the error of my omission. All I could do was stare stonily ahead with pathetic British reserve, whilst all around me Italians were exuberantly farting and belching and swilling wine from the bottle. And then the Adonis to the left offered me a swig, and a bite of his bread and salami. I snatched at both with no shame and we struck up an immediate rapport – until his wife took exception, swapping places with him after stamping on his open-toed sandals with her stiletto, and swiping him a swift blow with the rest of her big loaf. He sat for the rest of the show in a shower of breadcrumbs, cowering. But I couldn't have cared less, he'd catered to my needs and taught me a lesson which I've benefited from ever since. Never meddle with Italian men, unless they're out of sight of their womenfolk (Italian mamas are easily as possessive as their missuses', if not more).*

*I became a dab hand at open-air theatre catering after that. I saved the day, or rather the evening, when we'd gone to see a cliff-top production of Thornton Wilder's 'Our Town' (**totally** inappropriate choice of play for a Cornish setting). It was not only freezing, but raining into the bargain. But the cast soldiered on, and we were alright, cocooned in our raincapes – the inner man warmed by one of my best broths. Each thermos outrageously laced with Napoleon brandy. And, though I say it myself, I can claim to have done many parties proud down at Glyndebourne in my time. Though at Glyndebourne my attention usually focuses on the female programme sellers. I always idly wonder which, if any, are having it off with any of the male opera stars. My best friend had a whole summer-long affair with **the** singer that year (who shall, of course, remain nameless!). She was a fellow art student and selling programmes as a vacation job, eighteen, the same as me. And I was sick with chagrin, still a virgin, with every chance of remaining that way. My* *summer job was selling ice-creams at the Brighton Odeon, the seasonal hit there was Walt Disney's The Living Desert. Hard to get off on the mating habits of mosquitoes, especially knowing that SHE would be ringing me next morning with breathy whispers of what had gone on the night before in the wings . . .*

*And not just in the wings – the audience was crammed too with male glamour, so she claimed. Gilded youths, just the sort that I had always gone for. With sports cars and never a second glance in my direction. The very best of Britain, public school and all that. Shades of 'Brideshead Revisited'. Impossibly unattainable. You see them around still. In fact, I see them around all the time now with my daughters, reminders of those years of unrequited yearning.*

*We photographed Fred and Dominic, two of their chums, because to me they typify just what I mean. Beautiful Bambis, with the special bloom of youth, but unaware of their appeal. The setting is the Open Air Theatre in Regents Park. They are quaffing champagne. Of course, what else! And nibbling on delicacies dictated by Topsy.*

*When Johnny showed them the Polaroid test snap he'd taken first, neither seemed very impressed. 'Mm,' drawled young Dominic. 'I don't think much of us. Look like a couple of public school wets.' We remained silent, Johnny and me, feeling ancient and, yes – ugly. Beauty* **is** *in the eye of the beholder. Don't care what you say.*

## HOT CURRIED CHICKEN

- 1 teaspoonful curry paste
- 1 dessertspoonful mayonnaise
- 1/4 onion, finely chopped
- 1 teaspoonful mango chutney
- Salt and freshly ground black pepper
- A few drops of lemon juice
- 1/2 teaspoonful turmeric powder
- 2 slices of bread or 1 roll
- Butter
- Mayonnaise
- 2-3 pieces of cooked chicken, drumsticks or wing
- 2-3 slices of tomato
- 1-2 crisp lettuce leaves

Make the curry sauce by lightly mixing together the curry paste, mayonnaise, onion, mango chutney, salt, pepper, lemon juice and turmeric. Butter both slices of bread or halves of role. Spread one slice or half with mayonnaise and place the chicken on top. Heap the curry sauce on top and cover with the tomato, lettuce leaves and the second slice of bread or half of roll.

## CHICKEN AND AVOCADO

*2 slices of bread*
*Butter*
*1-2 slices of cooked chicken breast*
*A pinch of chicken seasoning*
*¼ avocado, peeled and sliced*
*1 teaspoonful finely grated onion*
*A few drops of lemon juice*
*Salt and freshly ground black pepper*
*2-3 slices of cucumber*
*1-2 crisp lettuce leaves*

Butter both slices of bread. Place the chicken on one slice. Sprinkle on the chicken seasoning. Then mix the mashed avocado together with the onion and lemon juice. Pile this mixture onto the chicken and season to taste. Cover with the cucumber and lettuce leaves. Top with the second slice of bread.

## TURKEY AND CRANBERRY SAUCE

*2 slices of bread*
*Butter*
*Mayonnaise*
*1-2 slices of cooked turkey breast*
*1 heaped teaspoonful cranberry sauce*
*2-3 slices of cucumber*
*Salt and freshly ground black pepper*
*1-2 crisp lettuce leaves*

Butter both slices of bread. Spread one slice with mayonnaise and lay the turkey on top. Cover with cranberry sauce and cucumber and season to taste. Cover with the lettuce leaves and top with the second slice of bread.

## DEVILLED TURKEY

*2 slices of bread*
*Butter*
*3-4 thin slices of cooked turkey leg*
*1 teaspoonful finely chopped onion*
*A dash of Worcestershire sauce*
*A dash of Tabasco sauce*
*1 teaspoonful chopped peppers*
*Salt and freshly ground black pepper*
*1 dessertspoonful mayonnaise*
*¼ tomato, thinly sliced*
*1-2 crisp lettuce leaves*

Butter both slices of bread. Place the turkey on one slice. Mix together the onion, Worcestershire and Tabasco sauces, peppers, seasoning and mayonnaise. Pile on top of the turkey and top with the tomato and lettuce. Cover with the second slice of bread.

# LIVER SAUSAGE AND APPLE

2 slices of bread
Butter
English mustard
25 g/1 oz liver sausage, mashed
1 teaspoonful finely chopped onion
1 heaped dessertspoonful soured cream
A few drops of brandy
1 good pinch of celery salt
2-3 slices of tart eating apple, cored
A sprinkling of lemon juice
Salt and freshly ground black pepper
1-2 crisp lettuce leaves
Mayonnaise

Butter both slices of bread. Spread one slice with mustard. Mix the liver sausage with the onion, soured cream, brandy and celery salt, making the mixture fairly moist. Spread this mixture fairly thickly on top of the mustard. Thinly slice the apple. Cover with the apple and sprinkle with lemon juice. Season with salt and pepper to taste and top with the lettuce leaves. Spread mayonnaise on the second slice of bread and cover the sandwich.

# GAMMON AND MUSHROOM WITH CHEESE

2 slices of bread or 1 roll or
1 15-cm/6-in piece of French stick
Butter
Grain mustard
1-2 thin slices of cooked gammon
25 g/1 oz Gruyère cheese, grated
2-3 flat mushrooms, cooked
1-2 onion rings, finely chopped
Salt and freshly ground black pepper
A pinch of paprika pepper
1/4 tomato, thinly sliced
1-2 crisp lettuce leaves
Mayonnaise

Butter both slices of bread or halves of roll or stick. Spread one slice with mustard and cover this with the gammon slices, cheese, mushrooms, onion rings and season with salt and pepper to taste and a pinch of paprika. Top with the tomato and lettuce leaves. Spread the second slice of bread or roll or stick with mayonnaise and cover the sandwich. This is also delicious toasted.

## BACON AND MUSHROOM

- 2-3 rashers of streaky bacon
- 2 slices of bread
- Butter
- Mayonnaise
- 1-2 flat mushrooms, cooked
- 1/4 clove of garlic, crushed
- 1-2 slices of tomato
- Salt and freshly ground black pepper
- 1 sprig of watercress
- 1-2 crisp lettuce leaves
- English or grain mustard

Remove the rinds from the bacon and cook it crisply. Drain it well. Butter both slices of bread. Spread one slice with mayonnaise and cover with the bacon, mushrooms, garlic and tomato. Season to taste. Add the watercress and lettuce. Spread the second slice of bread with mustard and cover the sandwich.

## TONGUE WITH APPLE AND RED CABBAGE

- 2 slices of bread
- Butter
- Mayonnaise
- 1-2 slices of cooked lamb's tongue
- 1/2 tart eating apple, peeled and finely sliced
- 25 g/1 oz pickled cabbage, drained well
- 1 teaspoonful chopped fresh chives
- 1 dessertspoonful mayonnaise
- Salt and freshly ground black pepper
- 1-2 crisp lettuce leaves
- English or grain mustard

Butter both slices of bread. Spread mayonnaise onto one slice and place the tongue on top. Mix the apple, cabbage and chives into the second quantity of mayonnaise and place on top. Season to taste and cover with the lettuce. Spread the second slice of bread with mustard and cover the sandwich.

## ROLLMOPS

- 2 slices of bread or 1 roll
- Butter
- Mayonnaise
- 1-2 small rollmops, flattened out and drained
- 2-3 thin slices of cucumber
- 1-2 sprigs of watercress
- 2-3 onion rings
- 1-2 crisp lettuce leaves

Butter both slices of bread or halves of roll and spread mayonnaise thickly on one slice of bread or half of roll. Cover with the rollmops, cucumber, watercress, onion and lettuce leaves. Cover with the second slice of bread or half of roll.

## TUNA, AVOCADO AND LUMPA FISH

- 2 slices of bread
- Butter
- 1 dessertspoonful mashed avocado
- A sprinkling of lemon juice
- 1 dessertspoonful tuna fish in brine, well drained
- 1 teaspoonful mayonnaise
- A pinch of cayenne pepper
- 2-3 thin slices of cucumber
- 1 heaped teaspoonful lumpa fish, washed and drained
- Freshly ground black pepper
- 1-2 crisp lettuce leaves
- 1 dessertspoonful creamed cheese

Butter both slices of bread. Sprinkle the mashed avocado with lemon juice. Mix the tuna fish with the mayonnaise and cayenne pepper. Pile onto one slice of bread and top with the avocado, cucumber, lumpa fish and black pepper. Top with the lettuce leaves. Spread the second slice of bread with the creamed cheese and cover the sandwich.

## GARLIC PRAWNS

- 2 slices of bread
- Butter
- 1 tablespoonful peeled prawns
- 1 tablespoonful mayonnaise
- 1/4 clove of garlic, crushed
- A dash of lemon juice
- A pinch of cayenne pepper
- A pinch of salt
- 2-3 thin slices of cucumber
- 1-2 crisp lettuce leaves

Butter both slices of bread. Mix together the prawns, mayonnaise, garlic, lemon juice, cayenne pepper and salt. Pile on one slice of bread and top with the cucumber and lettuce leaves. Cover with the second slice of bread.

## CRABMEAT AND ANCHOVY

- 2 slices of bread
- Butter
- 1 tablespoonful crabmeat, fresh or frozen
- 2-3 anchovy fillets in oil, well drained
- 1 small hardboiled egg
- 1 heaped teaspoonful mayonnaise
- Freshly ground black pepper
- 1-2 lettuce leaves

Butter both slices of bread. Place the crabmeat on one slice and top with the anchovy fillets. Mash the egg with the mayonnaise and pepper. Spread on top of the crabmeat and anchovies. Cover with the lettuce and top with the second slice of bread.

## FISH WITH ROQUEFORT OR BLUE CHEESE

1 tablespoonful any leftover cooked white fish
1 dessertspoonful single cream
Salt and freshly ground black pepper
15 g/½ oz Roquefort or Blue cheese
15 g/½ oz cream cheese
A few drops of brandy
A pinch of cayenne pepper
1-2 slices of tomato
1-2 crisp lettuce leaves
Mayonnaise

Butter both slices of bread. Bone and flake the fish. Mix the fish, cream, salt and pepper together and spread on the first slice of bread. Mix both cheeses with the brandy and cayenne pepper and spread this over the fish. Top with the tomato and lettuce leaves. Spread the second slice of bread with mayonnaise and cover the sandwich.

## GOUDA AND APPLES WITH WALNUTS

2 slices of bread
Butter
Grain mustard
2-3 thickish slices Gouda cheese
2-3 slices tart apple, unpeeled
1 heaped teaspoonful of chopped walnuts
1-2 crisp lettuce leaves
Mayonnaise

Butter both slices of bread. Spread one slice with grain mustard and cover with the cheese, apple, walnuts and lettuce leaves. Spread the second slice of bread with mayonnaise and cover the sandwich.

## MOZZARELLA, ARTICHOKES AND SALAMI

2 slices of bread
Butter
4-5 1-cm/¼-in slices of Mozzarella
1-2 artichoke hearts, broken up
2-3 slices of salami
2-3 slices of tomato
A pinch of mixed herbs
2-3 crisp lettuce leaves
Mayonnaise

Butter both slices of bread. Cover one slice with the Mozzarella, artichokes, salami and tomato and sprinkle with mixed herbs. Top with the lettuce leaves. Spread mayonnaise on the second slice of bread and close the sandwich.

# Office Lunch Box

*I'd always wanted to work in an office, preferably as a secretary, with a chance to make eyes at the boss. And then marry him. The fiction I read in women's magazines, as a girl, was all about that sort of thing. I thought what a* **positive** *sense of power it must give you to make yourself so indispensable to the man at the top, that if you had to take the afternoon off because you'd broken both wrists and lost the sight of one eye (a good secretary is* **not** *a malingerer and would never take more than the afternoon) the place would grind to a standstill – and lead inevitably to a proposal of marriage.*

*It never occurred to me until many, many years later, that having a secretary – being the boss yourself – gives a sense of power too. Not quite the same, because when you're the boss there's nowhere to go. Only down. Which triggers off more anxieties than being on the upward spiral. I know because I've been in both places. What we're talking about here is naked ambition.* **You** *know, girls. About* **getting on**.

*It's interesting to me, when I look back on the kids who, since I first met them, have 'made it'. I knew little Mikey Fleetwood when he was nine. 'And what do you want to be when you grow up?' I asked him in that infuriatingly patronizing way that adults employ when addressing children. But his answer came promptly, no hesitation, 'I shall be,' he piped without bombast, 'the best drummer in the world.' 'Oh, really?' 'You wait and see,' he smiled back at me. Mick Fleetwood, of Fleetwood Mac, one of the most successful groups in the whole world!*

*Zandra Rhodes was the same, no doubt in her mind as to where she was headed. Though who could have guessed what a prodigious capacity for hard work she has. Success is never a question of mere talent. And Bette Midler, whom I met before she hit international headlines. If her energy had not been so totally exhilarating, I'd have needed a wheelchair from sheer exhaustion.*

*There is an aura about those for whom success lies in wait, one of which only they are fully aware sometimes. I have rarely, if ever, seen anyone with that aura fail. Sometimes, interviewing an unknown on the pages of 'The Sunday Times', thereby bringing them into the public eye, I was accused of forcing the hand of fate. It was pointed out to me that by stating in print that this youngster would become known in their particular field, I was already making sure of that.*

*Bianca Jagger had never been interviewed before we did a fashion spread on her, for instance. And Steve Strange had still to cut his first album, or be taken as a charismatic influence to be reckoned seriously by the press, when I first wrote about him. But I maintained, and still do, that it's all a question of time. In the end that recognition would have come anyway. All I ever did was escalate the process.*

*Sara Sugarman, whom I chose for our Office Lunch Box snap, is very much a case in point. She's an actress, a comedienne – meaning to say that she can as swiftly make you laugh as bring a lump to the throat. The best sort, a special girl in my opinion, with the aura that I've mentioned. Anyway, I'm willing to chance my arm on her, though she's only just twenty-one (at the time of going to print) and just at the start of things yet. But watch out for her, that's all. She'd tell you herself. 'You're all set for stardom, aren't you?' I said, stating a fact one evening. 'Of course I am, can you tell?' 'Stands out a mile, kid.' She nodded, no need to say anything else.*

*'D'you fancy posing for our Office Lunch Box photo, Sara?' I phoned her that same week. 'It's for a book on sandwiches. I'd like you as a sexy secretary, OK?'*

*'Why do I have to be somebody's secretary? Why can't I be the boss? Bosses eat lunch in the office too, y'know.' Of course. Right on, kid. Yes, point taken!*

*'Though if you want me as a secretary,' she added quickly, 'I expect I could get in drag.' 'It'll be experience. In front of the camera, I mean. And you'll be putting my name in print . . .'*

*Sara arrived* **before me** *at the studio! All ready to start, make-up, the leather skirt, hair slicked back – the lot!*

*'This kid's on the ball, isn't she?' Johnny hadn't met her before. 'Going places, wouldn't you say, Moll?'*

*'Going places.* **For sure**.*'*

## ROAST LAMB AND JELLY

- 2 slices of bread or 1 roll
- Butter
- 2 slices roast lamb
- 1 dessertspoonful redcurrant or mint jelly
- 1/4 cucumber, thinly sliced
- 1-2 crisp lettuce leaves
- Salt and freshly ground black pepper
- Mayonnaise

Spread the slices of bread or halves of roll with butter. Put the roast lamb onto one slice of bread or one half of roll and top with the redcurrant or mint jelly, cucumber and lettuce. Sprinkle with salt and pepper. Cover the second slice of bread or half of roll with a little mayonnaise and close the sandwich.

## ROAST LAMB AND APRICOT

- 2 slices of bread
- Butter
- 1 tinned apricot, drained
- 2-3 slices roast lamb
- Salt and freshly ground black pepper
- 4-5 thin slices of cucumber
- 1-2 crisp lettuce leaves
- Mayonnaise

Butter both slices of bread. Slice the apricot finely. Add the lamb to one slice of bread and cover with the apricot. Add the seasoning, then the cucumber and lettuce. Spread a thin layer of mayonnaise on the second slice of bread and cover the sandwich.

## ROAST BEEF WITH CHEESE

- 2 slices of bread
- Butter
- English mustard
- 1-2 good slices rare roast beef
- A sprinkling of chopped, hardboiled egg
- A sprinkling of chopped celery
- 1 small teaspoonful mayonnaise
- Salt and freshly ground black pepper
- 1 small teaspoonful Parmesan cheese
- 1-2 crisp lettuce leaves

*Spread the slices of bread with butter. Spread the mustard on one slice and cover with the roast beef. Mix the egg and celery together with the mayonnaise and pile onto the beef. Season to taste and sprinkle on the Parmesan cheese liberally. Cover with lettuce leaves and top with the second slice of bread. This is also good toasted.*

## SALT BEEF

- 2 slices of bread
- Butter
- Grain mustard
- 2 slices of salt beef, cut into slivers
- ½ tomato, sliced
- Salt and freshly ground black pepper
- 1-2 crisp lettuce leaves
- 1 teaspoonful horseradish sauce

*Butter both slices of bread. Spread grain mustard on one of the slices. Lay the beef on top of the mustard and cover with the tomato, seasoning and lettuce. Spread the horseradish sauce on the second slice of bread and cover.*

## HAM WITH VEGETABLES

- 2 slices of bread
- Butter
- French mustard
- 50 g/2 oz mixed grated carrots, onions and pepper
- Mayonnaise
- 1 dessertspoonful of salt and black pepper
- 2 slices of ham
- 1-2 crisp lettuce leaves

*Spread both slices of bread with butter and mustard. Mix the grated vegetables with the mayonnaise and season to taste. Cover one slice of bread with the ham and heap the vegetables on top. Cover with the lettuce leaves and the second slice of bread.*

## PORK WITH CELERY AND MOZZARELLA

- 2 slices of bread
- Butter
- English or grain mustard to taste
- 2-3 slices of roast pork
- 1 small stick of celery, diced
- 3-4 1-cm/¼-in slices of Mozzarella cheese
- 3 thin slices of cucumber
- Salt and freshly ground black pepper
- 1-2 crisp lettuce leaves
- Mayonnaise

Butter both slices of bread. Spread mustard on one slice. Cover one slice with the pork and top with the celery, Mozzarella and cucumber. Season to taste and cover with the lettuce. Spread mayonnaise on the second slice of bread and cover the sandwich.

## GANNET'S SPECIAL

- 3-4 chicken livers
- 1 15-cm/6-in piece of French stick
- Butter
- Grain mustard
- ½ tomato, sliced
- 1 thick slice of corned beef
- 1 teaspoonful finely chopped onion
- 2 slices Italian salami, skin removed
- 2-3 slices cucumber
- 1-2 crisp lettuce leaves
- Sprig of watercress
- Mayonnaise

Cook the chicken livers in a small amount of butter until the outsides have changed colour and the insides are still slightly pink. Be careful not to overcook them. Chop them into small pieces. Cut the bread in half and butter both sides. Spread mustard on one side and top with the chicken livers, tomato, corned beef and onion; then follow with the salami, cucumber, lettuce and sprig of watercress. Spread the second side of bread with mayonnaise and cover.

## CHICKEN, SPINACH, TOMATO AND CHEESE

- 2 slices of bread
- Butter
- 3-4 slices of cooked chicken breast
- 2-3 slices of tomato
- Salt and freshly ground black pepper
- 25 g/1 oz grated Cheddar cheese
- 1-2 spinach leaves
- Mayonnaise

Butter both slices of bread. Place the chicken breasts on one slice and cover with the tomato. Season to taste and top with the grated cheese and spinach leaves. Spread the second slice of bread with mayonnaise and cover the sandwich.

## EGG WITH SPINACH AND GARLIC

- 2 slices of bread or 1 roll
- Butter
- 2 hardboiled eggs, chopped
- Salt and freshly ground black pepper
- 1 dessertspoonful mayonnaise
- 1 tablespoonful cooked spinach, well drained
- 1/4 small clove garlic, crushed
- 1-2 crisp lettuce leaves

*Butter the slices of bread or both halves of roll. Mix the hardboiled eggs with salt and pepper and the mayonnaise. Chop the spinach and mix the garlic with it. Pile the egg mixture onto one slice of bread or half of roll, cover with the spinach mixture and top with the lettuce leaves. Cover with the second slice of bread or half of roll.*

## SALMON AND CREAM CHEESE

- 2 slices of bread
- Butter
- 1 tablespoonful tinned salmon, well drained
- A pinch of cayenne pepper
- A few drops of lemon juice
- Salt and freshly ground black pepper
- 1 dessertspoonful cream cheese
- 1 dessertspoonful celery, finely chopped
- 2-3 thin slices of cucumber
- 1-2 crisp lettuce leaves
- Mayonnaise

*Butter both slices of bread. Mash the salmon with cayenne pepper, lemon juice and seasoning. Spread on top of one slice of bread and top with the cream cheese, celery, cucumber and lettuce. Spread mayonnaise on the second slice of bread and cover the sandwich.*

## SMOKED HADDOCK WITH HORSERADISH

- 1/2 small smoked haddock
- 2 slices of bread
- Butter
- Mayonnaise
- 1 dessertspoonful horseradish sauce
- A few drops of lemon juice
- Freshly ground black pepper
- 2-3 wafer-thin slices of cucumber
- 1-2 crisp lettuce leaves

*Cook the haddock in a small amount of milk with a knob of butter. Drain, cool and mash the fish. Butter the bread and spread thinly with mayonnaise. Mix the haddock and horseradish together with a few drops of lemon juice and some pepper. Spread the mixture on the first slice of bread and cover with the cucumber and lettuce leaves. Cover with the second slice of bread.*

## SEAFOOD SPECIAL

- 2 slices of bread
- Butter
- 1 tablespoonful tuna fish in brine, drained
- 1 hardboiled egg, chopped
- 1/4 onion, finely chopped
- A dash of cayenne pepper
- 6 mussels, cooked and shelled
- 4 shelled prawns
- Pinch of salt
- 1 tablespoonful mayonnaise
- 2 anchovy fillets in oil, well drained
- A few drops of lemon juice
- 1-2 crisp lettuce leaves

Spread the slices of bread with butter. Drain the tuna fish well. Mix the hardboiled egg with the onion, cayenne pepper, mussels, tuna fish, prawns, salt and mayonnaise and pile the mixture onto one slice of bread. Top with the anchovy fillets and sprinkle with lemon juice. Cover with lettuce leaves and the second slice.

## SPICY SARDINE

- 2 slices of bread
- Butter
- 2-3 sardines in oil, well drained
- A dash of Tabasco sauce
- 1/4 clove of garlic, crushed
- A dash of Worcestershire sauce
- A pinch of dill
- 1 teaspoonful chopped peppers
- Salt and freshly ground black pepper
- 1 dessertspoonful mayonnaise
- 1-2 thin slices of cucumber
- 1-2 crisp lettuce leaves

Butter both slices of bread. Mix together the sardines, Tabasco sauce, garlic, Worcestershire sauce, dill, peppers, seasoning and mayonnaise. Spread this mixture on one slice of bread and top with the cucumber and lettuce. Cover with the second slice of bread.

## EMMENTHAL CHEESE AND GREEN PEPPERS

*2 slices of bread or 1 roll*
*Butter*
*2 slices Emmenthal cheese*
*2 slices green pepper*
*¼ cucumber, sliced*
*½ tomato, sliced*
*1-2 crisp lettuce leaves*
*English mustard*
*1 teaspoonful mayonnaise*

*Butter the slices of bread or halves of roll. Cover one slice or half with the cheese, pepper, cucumber, tomato and lettuce. Spread the second slice of bread or half of roll with mustard and mayonnaise and place on top of the first slice or half. This is good for slimmers.*

## COTTAGE CHEESE WITH WALNUTS

*2 slices of bread or 1 roll*
*Butter*
*1 tablespoonful cottage cheese*
*1 heaped teaspoonful chopped walnuts*
*A sprinkling of chopped, fresh chives*
*Salt and freshly ground black pepper*
*1-2 crisp lettuce leaves*

*Spread the slices of bread or halves of roll with butter. Cover one slice or half with the cottage cheese, walnuts and freshly chopped chives. Season with salt and pepper and top with the lettuce leaves. Close the sandwich with the second slice of bread or half of roll. This is good for slimmers.*

## GRUYERE AND PINEAPPLE

*2 slices of bread*
*Butter*
*1-2 pineapple rings, fresh or tinned*
*Mayonnaise for spreading*
*3-4 medium slices of Gruyère cheese*
*A sprinkling of celery salt or*
*1 small stick of fresh celery, diced*
*Salt and freshly ground black pepper*
*1-2 crisp lettuce leaves*

*Butter both slices of bread. If using tinned pineapple, drain well. Spread mayonnaise on one slice and cover with the Gruyère cheese, pineapple and celery. Season to taste and add the lettuce leaves. Top with the second slice of bread.*

# POINT TO POINT

*We shot our Point to Point pictures at Whipsnade Zoo, or was it Chessington? They all used to seem exactly the same to me when I was taken as a child. I thought all zoos were horrible. I'd cry myself to sleep at night afterwards, thinking of lions and tigers behind bars. And elephants with tiny, unhappy eyes doing tricks with their trunks for bun treats. I can't ever recall one nice outing to the zoo, not even when I took my own children. It always seemed to end up with quarrels. With a lot of queueing at the café for cold sausage rolls and the sort of cakes that even the elephant would have turned his elongated nose up at.*

*Now fairgrounds were a different matter altogether. Nobody with red blood coursing through their veins could not thrill to the fever-pitch excitement of a fairground. Which is how we happened to find ourselves at – yes, it was Chessington Zoo. Theirs was the only fairground we could find open when we were searching for merry-go-round horses at the end of the summer. And I had set my mind on fairground horses, in place of the real thing.*

*It's not that I have anything against real-life horses as such, though I can't honestly claim to having met any. Where on earth would I have met them? I never went down the coal mines back home as a child. If I had done I could have struck up a passing acquaintance with a pit pony, perhaps. Poor little blighters. And it's certainly true that there were wild horses up there on the top of the mountains. But never a single one came nuzzling to my tiny fist for a sugar lump. Besides, if I'd been carrying sugar lumps all that way to the very top I most certainly would have scoffed them by the time I reached there.*

*Yet I was as eager as everyone else to see 'National Velvet' when it came out. And I entertained the same dreams as any other little girl, to have my own horse and go riding. Or were those just social aspirations of the snobbish sort. Probably. Yes. I own up.*

*I own up, too, to being over the moon when one of my many fiancés (this one I actually got around to marrying – he was to become my first husband) invited me to go to what turned out to be my first and very last point to point.*

*I don't remember too much about the car journey there, nothing much about the conversation, which was all horsey talk. But I knew from that start that the only salvation for me, if I was to last the full horror of the day, was to get well and truly sloshed.*

*My clothes were all wrong. I looked – not quite the part. In truth I looked hideously out of place all in black, with my existentialist chalk-white face (real chalk mixed with a box of face powder from Woolies) and kohl-rimmed eyes. If the horses had seen me they would have run from sheer fright in the other direction.*

*I do remember the food, though I was mostly impressed by the size of the Harrods' hamper as much as the contents. Oh, how endearingly provincial I was in those days, how diffident, how difficult, how painfully class-conscious. How cruelly critical of social mores and manners with which I couldn't cope. I think now that my first young husband deserved a medal for polishing –* **so many** *rough edges on this particular pebble!*

*And so (you understand the reasoning!) we shot the Point to Point photograph on the most decorative horse we could find at the Chessington Zoo merry-go-round, in jokey place of the real live thing. All that was lacking was a horse's mouth to put the sandwich in – no one had thought of that! So young Jimmy, the fairground help, sweetly offered his services. That's his grubby little paw, there in the photo. Johnny was horrified. 'Hardly hygienic! Look at the state of his nails – we'll have readers complaining.' 'We're not asking the readers to eat out of Jimmy's hand, Johnny.' I pointed out, mildly enough I would have said. But we'd already had the teensiest, weensiest, contretemps over which horse we should use and at which specific angle. Added to which I'd promised Jimmy he could eat the sandwich once we'd finished the photo. Johnny had been looking forward to it himself. Topsy's special filling was his favourite.* **Not** *one of our better days! But no surprise. When had I* **ever** *enjoyed anything to do with point to points – or zoos?*

## RARE BEEF WITH HORSERADISH

2 slices of bread
Butter
1-2 slices rare beef
½ tomato, sliced
1 sprig of watercress
Salt and freshly ground black pepper
1-2 crisp lettuce leaves
Horseradish sauce, preferably home-made

Butter both slices of bread. Place the beef and tomato on one slice, top with the watercress and season to taste. Cover with the lettuce. Spread horseradish sauce onto the second slice of bread and cover the sandwich.

## FILLET STEAK

1 small fillet steak
2 slices of brown bread
Butter
Grain mustard
2-3 flat mushrooms, cooked and drained
¼ clove of garlic, crushed
½ tomato, sliced
Salt and freshly ground black pepper
1-2 crisp lettuce leaves
Mayonnaise

Beat the fillet steak and cook it rare. Butter both slices of bread. Spread grain mustard on one slice and cover with the fillet steak, mushrooms, garlic and tomato. Season to taste and cover with the lettuce leaves. Spread the second slice of bread with mayonnaise and cover the sandwich. Cook until crisp in a preheated oven (200°C, 400°F, Gas Mark 6), or under the grill.

## HAMBURGER AND BLUE CHEESE

- 75 g/3 oz minced beef
- 2 slices of bread
- Oil or melted butter
- Pinch of mixed herbs
- Salt and freshly ground black pepper
- 1 dessertspoonful cucumber chutney
- 1 heaped dessertspoonful Blue cheese, crumbled
- 2-3 flat mushrooms, cooked

Lightly cook the mince and knead it into a flat 'cake', approximately the same shape as the bread. Brush both slices of bread with oil or melted butter on one side. Place the meat on the dry surface of one slice of bread. Add the herbs and seasoning. Spread the cucumber chutney on top and add the cheese and mushrooms. Cover with second slice of bread, dry side downwards and cook in a preheated oven, 200°C, 400°F, Gas Mark 6, or under the grill until crisp.

## LIVER, PIMENTOS AND ASPARAGUS

- 2 slices of bread
- Butter
- 1 dessertspoonful mayonnaise
- 2-3 thin slices lamb's liver, cooked
- 2-3 thin slices red pimentos
- 4-6 asparagus tips
- 25 g/1 oz farmhouse cheese, grated
- Salt and freshly ground black pepper
- 1 sprig of watercress
- French mustard

Butter both slices of bread. Spread one slice of bread with mayonnaise. Top with the slices of liver, pimentos, asparagus and grated cheese. Season to taste and cover with the watercress. Spread French mustard on the second slice of bread and close the sandwich.

## PARMA HAM AND MELON

- 2 slices of bread
- Butter
- 3-4 wafer-thin slices of Parma ham
- Salt and freshly ground black pepper
- 2-3 thin slices of fresh melon
- 2-3 wafer-thin slices of cucumber
- 2-3 crisp lettuce leaves
- Mayonnaise

Butter both slices of bread. Lay the Parma ham on one slice and season to taste. Top with the melon, cucumber and lettuce leaves. Spread mayonnaise on the second slice of bread and cover the sandwich.

## HAM AND PEACH CHUTNEY

- 2 slices of bread or 1 roll
- Butter
- 2 slices ham
- 1/4 cucumber, sliced
- 1 dessertspoonful peach chutney
- Salt and freshly ground black pepper
- 1-2 crisp lettuce leaves
- English mustard
- Mayonnaise

Butter the slices of bread or halves of roll. Put the ham onto one slice of bread or one half of roll. Put the cucumber and the peach chutney onto the centre of the ham, sprinkle with salt and pepper and cover with the lettuce leaves. Spread the second slice of bread with mustard and mayonnaise and cover the sandwich.

## TURKEY WITH SAVOURY PASTE

- 2 slices of bread
- Butter
- 1 dessertspoonful chopped, cooked mushrooms
- 1 dessertspoonful chopped, fried onion
- A pinch of dried sage
- 1 teaspoonful of mayonnaise
- 50 g/2 oz thinly sliced cooked turkey breast
- Freshly ground black pepper
- 3-4 slices of tomato
- 1-2 crisp lettuce leaves

Butter both slices of bread. Mix together the mushrooms, onions and sage and bind with the mayonnaise. Place the turkey meat on one slice. Smooth the mushroom paste over the turkey and add the pepper. Place the tomato and lettuce on top and then cover with the remaining slice of bread.

## DUCK IN PORT WITH GREEN OLIVES

- 2 slices of roast duck breast
- 1 dessertspoonful of port
- 2 slices of bread
- Butter
- 6 green olives, halved and stoned
- Salt and freshly ground black pepper
- A pinch of paprika
- 3-4 slices of tomato
- 1-2 crisp lettuce leaves
- Mayonnaise

Marinate the duck overnight in the port. Butter both slices of bread. Remove the duck from the marinade and drain. Arrange the slices of duck on one piece of bread and cover with the olives. Add the seasoning and paprika. Cover with the tomato and lettuce. Spread mayonnaise on the second slice of bread and close the sandwich.

## DUCK WITH PINEAPPLE AND HONEY

*2 slices of bread*
*Butter*
*Clear honey*
*2 slices of pineapple*
*2 thick slices of duck breast*
*Salt and freshly ground black pepper*
*4-5 thin slices of cucumber*
*1-2 crisp lettuce leaves*

*Butter both slices of bread. Spread a thin layer of clear honey on each slice. If using tinned pineapple, drain well. Arrange the duck slices on one slice of bread and cover with the pineapple. Season to taste, then add the cucumber and the lettuce leaves. Top with the second slice of bread.*

## PHEASANT WITH CHESTNUT STUFFING

*2 slices of bread*
*Butter*
*3-4 thin slices of cooked pheasant*
*1 dessertspoonful chestnut stuffing*
*1/4 tomato, thinly sliced*
*1-2 crisp lettuce leaves*
*Mayonnaise*

*Butter both slices of bread. Lay the pheasant on one slice of bread, and top with the stuffing, tomato and lettuce. Spread the second slice of bread with mayonnaise and cover the sandwich.*

## PHEASANT WITH BLACK GRAPES

*2 slices of bread*
*Butter*
*1 teaspoonful chicken liver pâté*
*3 thin slices cooked pheasant breast*
*6 black grapes, halved and pips removed*
*4-5 thin slices of cucumber*
*Salt and freshly ground black pepper*
*1-2 crisp lettuce leaves*

*Butter both slices of bread. Then spread the pâté on both buttered surfaces. Place the pheasant, grapes and cucumber on top of one slice and season to taste. Cover with the lettuce leaves and top with the second slice of bread.*

## CRAB

2 slices of bread
Butter
1 tablespoonful crabmeat, either fresh or frozen
1 dessertspoonful mayonnaise
Salt and freshly ground black pepper
A pinch of cayenne pepper
A sprinkling of lemon juice
2-3 wafer-thin slices of cucumber
1-2 crisp lettuce leaves

Butter both slices of bread. If using frozen crabmeat, allow it to thaw first. Mix the crabmeat with the mayonnaise, salt, pepper and cayenne pepper. Pile onto the first slice of bread. Sprinkle with lemon juice and top with cucumber and lettuce. Cover with the second slice of bread.

## SMOKED HADDOCK IN CHEESE

1 small smoked haddock fillet, cooked
1 dessertspoonful grated mature Cheddar
1 hardboiled egg, sliced
1 dessertspoonful mayonnaise
Freshly ground black pepper
1/4 tomato, sliced
1-2 crisp lettuce leaves

Butter both slices of bread. Skin the haddock fillet. Mash the haddock together with the cheese and egg in the mayonnaise. Season with pepper to taste. Pile this mixture onto one slice of bread. Top with the tomato and lettuce leaves and cover the sandwich with the second slice of bread.

## SHRIMP AND TUNA COCKTAIL

2 slices of bread
Butter
1 dessertspoonful peeled shrimps
1 dessertspoonful tuna in brine, well drained
2-3 flat mushrooms, cooked and chopped
1 teaspoonful chopped, hardboiled egg
1 teaspoonful finely chopped onion
1-2 green olives, stoned and chopped
1-2 pieces of pimento, chopped
1 dessertspoonful mayonnaise
A sprinkling of lemon juice
2-3 thin slices of cucumber
1-2 crisp lettuce leaves

Butter both slices of bread. Mix the shrimps, tuna, mushrooms, egg, onion, olives and pimento with the mayonnaise and lemon juice. Spread on one slice of bread. Cover with the cucumber and lettuce and close the sandwich.

## MUSSELS WITH SAVOURY PASTE

- 2 slices of bread
- Butter
- 50 g/2 oz tinned mussels
- 1 teaspoonful chopped parsley
- 1/4 clove of garlic, crushed
- A pinch of paprika
- 1 dessertspoonful of mayonnaise
- 3-4 slices of tomato
- 1-2 crisp lettuce leaves

Butter both slices of bread. Mix together the mussels, parsley, garlic, paprika and mayonnaise. Spread this mixture on the first slice of bread and add the tomatoes and lettuce. Top with the remaining slice of bread.

## PRAWNS AND AVOCADO

- 1 teaspoonful mayonnaise
- A touch of tomato purée
- 1 teaspoonful double cream
- A few drops of brandy
- Salt and freshly ground black pepper
- 2 slices of bread
- Butter
- 1 heaped tablespoonful shelled prawns
- 1/2 avocado, peeled and sliced
- 1 teaspoonful finely grated onion
- 1-2 thin slices of cucumber
- 1-2 crisp lettuce leaves

Make the sauce for the prawns by mixing together the mayonnaise, tomato purée, double cream, brandy, salt and pepper. Butter both slices of bread. Mix the prawns with the prawn sauce and spread on one slice of bread. Top with the avocado, onion, cucumber and lettuce. Cover with the second slice of bread.

## AVOCADO WITH ROQUEFORT

- 2 slices of bread
- Butter
- 25 g/1 oz Roquefort cheese
- 15 g/1/2 oz butter, softened
- 25 g/1 oz white curd cheese, well drained
- Salt and freshly ground black pepper
- A pinch of paprika
- 1/4 ripe avocado
- A few drops of lemon juice
- 1-2 wafer-thin slices of cucumber
- 1-2 crisp lettuce leaves

Butter both slices of bread. Mix together the Roquefort cheese, butter, curd cheese, salt, pepper and a pinch of paprika. Spread this mixture on one slice of bread. Peel the avocado, remove the stone and mash it. Mix in the lemon juice. Pile the mashed avocado on top of the cheese mixture. Top with the cucumber and lettuce leaves. Cover with the second slice of bread.

# Non-Carnivores

*This section for Non-Carnivores is very close to my heart on two counts. Firstly, for the fact that I am now a vegetarian. The States did that for me, those king-size, plate-covering steaks they place before you turned me against meat for once and all. For a while I still ate fish, but not any more. On the tongue it seems to me still to be **flesh**, like consuming a creature from the animal kingdom. Which it is to my mind, but it's a purely personal matter. We are all of us allowed to eat what we want. Well – up to a point. Now the physicalities of that fact come into play, for much depends on our individual tools and equipment. To get down to basics, it's a question of whether or not you still have your own teeth. Or whether, like me, you're a card-carrying owner of dentures.*

*Little is written about specific food for those of us with false teeth, which is surprising when you consider just how many of us there are around. And when I talk of false teeth I don't just mean dentures for folk of a certain age. I'm talking about those who, for cosmetic purposes, have had their front teeth, and others, capped. Models, singers, young actors and actresses, all who wish to improve their appearance.*

*My front teeth are capped, four of them are. What I refer to as a denture is technically known as a plate, but the problems with food are the same. Blackberries are a nightmare, anything with pips or shreds or slivers that get stuck between palate and plate and can't easily be removed in polite company – but we'll come to polite company in a minute! Capped teeth are similarly hazardous. 'Apples are out!' snarled this New York dentist to me, irritably replacing a front cap that'd snapped off. 'And understand that your days of biting the head off a raw carrot – they're over too!' The replacing of broken caps is a costly procedure. I meekly succumbed to his command.*

*I have learned to live with my assortment of teeth, the home-grown and others. In fact, I've turned them into a positive advantage when it comes to choosing my company. The impolite sort is more my cup of tea, of course (surprise, surprise!). When I first met Bruce Lacey (how many hundreds of years ago was that?) I warmed to him on sight. He'd removed his top dentures to make an obscure point in the conversation. I removed mine to show social support. Now, on arrival at the same function, we wave our dentures to each other across a crowded room. Strangers cower and blanch, turn away in disgust. Those who know us set up a cheer of encouragement. We find it separates the wonderful from the wimps and weeds. It's called putting your infirmities to good use.*

*Bruce Lacey, artiste 'extraordinaire', inventor of robots, chosen even by eccentrics as one of **the** eccentrics of our time, has been a vegetarian since I don't known when. He **loves** sandwiches. They fit in with his curiously cockeyed existence down in Norfolk, where he's now chosen to reside. We photographed him at his anvil, his current obsession, in the iron-foundry barn alongside his back kitchen. A white goat bleated at the door, pleading a bit of Bruce's sandwich. No chance. Bruce gobbled it all himself, a rich combination of mushrooms, mashed eggs, mayonnaise, tomatoes, green peppers and lettuce on a soft, square bap. For the exercise he'd put his teeth back into his mouth (having removed them, as you see, for the snap!). We drove back to London, having hugged him goodbye, feeling sadly* *diminished at the loss of his company. 'That's the thing about our sandwich set,' I said in the silent car, 'they're life-enhancers, they're not afraid to make fools of themselves giving lots of laughs to others.'*

*'Show-offs, you mean,' said Johnny, shortly. 'Just like you.' I think he must have been worrying about whether he'd got the right exposure on the film and enough focus on the false teeth* ***and*** *the sandwich. That's all I could put it down to.*

## CURRIED EGG SALAD

- ½ teaspoonful curry paste
- 1 dessertspoonful mayonnaise
- ¼ onion, finely chopped
- 1 teaspoonful mango chutney
- Salt and freshly ground black pepper
- A few drops of lemon juice
- ½ teaspoonful turmeric powder
- 2 slices of bread or 1 roll
- Butter
- 1 hardboiled egg, roughly chopped
- ½ tomato, sliced
- 1-2 crisp lettuce leaves

Make the curry sauce by lightly mixing together the curry paste, mayonnaise, onion, mango chutney, salt, pepper, lemon juice and turmeric. Butter both slices of bread or halves of roll. Mix the egg into the curry sauce and spread onto the first slice of bread or half of roll. Cover with the tomato and lettuce and top with the second slice of bread or half of roll.

## EGG AND MUSHROOM

- 2 slices of bread or 1 roll
- Butter
- 1 egg, hardboiled or scrambled
- 1 dessertspoonful mayonnaise
- Salt and freshly ground black pepper
- 2 flat mushrooms, cooked and roughly chopped
- ½ tomato, sliced
- ¼ clove garlic, crushed
- 1-2 crisp lettuce leaves

Butter both slices of bread or halves of roll. If using hardboiled egg mash roughly and mix with the mayonnaise, salt and pepper. You do not need mayonnaise, salt and pepper if using scrambled egg. Pile this or the scrambled egg onto one slice of bread or half of roll and top with the mushrooms, tomato, garlic and lettuce and the second slice of bread or half of roll.

## ITALIAN SPECIAL

*1 15-cm/6-in piece of French stick*
*Butter*
*1 heaped teaspoonful mayonnaise*
*¼ clove of garlic, mashed*
*A few drops of lemon juice*
*25 g/1 oz Mozzarella cheese*
*1 tomato, thinly sliced*
*1 teaspoonful chopped onion*
*Pinch of mixed herbs*
*2-3 slices of cucumber*
*Good pinch of parsley*
*Salt and freshly ground black pepper*
*1-2 crisp lettuce leaves*

*Cut the French stick in half lengthways and butter both sides. Mix the mayonnaise with the garlic and lemon juice and spread on the first slice of bread. Top with the Mozzarella cheese, tomato, onion, mixed herbs and cucumber and sprinkle with chopped parsley. Season to taste. Cover with the lettuce leaves and the second half of bread.*

## BLUE CHEESE WITH BLACK GRAPES

*2 slices of bread*
*Butter*
*50 g/2 oz Danish Blue cheese, crumbled*
*3-4 slices of cucumber*
*6 black grapes, halved and pips removed*
*1-2 crisp lettuce leaves*

*Butter both slices of bread and then add the Blue cheese to one slice. Cover the cheese with the cucumber and then the grapes. Finally, add the lettuce leaves and top with the remaining slice of bread.*

## CREAM CHEESE AND CHIVES

*2 slices of bread or 1 roll*
*Butter*
*1 tablespoonful cream cheese*
*1 teaspoonful grated celery*
*1 teaspoonful grated carrot*
*½ teaspoonful sultanas*
*½ teaspoonful grated onion*
*Salt and freshly ground black pepper*
*1 dessertspoonful mayonnaise*
*1-2 crisp lettuce leaves*
*Grain mustard*

*Butter both slices of bread or halves of roll. Spread one slice of bread or half of roll thickly with the cream cheese. Mix together the celery, carrot, sultanas, onion, salt and pepper in the mayonnaise. Pile this mixture on top of the cheese. Cover with the lettuce leaves. Spread mustard on the second slice of bread or half of roll and close the sandwich.*

## CREAM CHEESE WITH NUTS AND FRUIT

- 2 slices of bread
- Butter
- 50 g/2 oz cream cheese
- 1 tablespoonful split almonds
- 1 dessertspoonful sultanas or raisins
- ½ crisp eating apple, thinly sliced
- 1-2 crisp lettuce leaves

Butter both slices of bread. Mix the cheese, almonds and sultanas together. Add the apple slices and lettuce and cover with the second slice of bread.

## GOAT CHEESE WITH CUCUMBER

- 2 slices bread or 1 roll
- Butter
- 2-3 slices Crottin (goat cheese)
- Salt and freshly ground black pepper
- 2-3 slices cucumber
- 1-2 young spinach leaves
- 1 black olive, stoned and sliced
- 1-2 crisp lettuce leaves
- ¼ clove of garlic, crushed
- ½ teaspoonful mayonnaise

Butter both slices of bread or halves of roll. Slice the Crottin thickly and place onto one piece of bread or half of roll. Season to taste and top with the cucumber, spinach leaves, olive and lettuce. Mix the garlic with the mayonnaise and spread on the second slice of bread or half of roll. Close the sandwich.

## COTTAGE CHEESE AND CARROT

- 2 slices of bread
- Butter
- 1 tablespoonful cottage cheese
- 1 dessertspoonful grated carrot
- 1 heaped teaspoonful Branston pickle
- Salt and freshly ground black pepper
- 1-2 large sprigs of watercress
- Mayonnaise

Butter both slices of bread. Spread the cottage cheese on one slice and pile on the carrot and Branston pickle. Season to taste and top with the watercress. Spread mayonnaise on the second slice of bread and close the sandwich.

## SAVOURY CHEDDAR WITH APPLE

- 2 slices of bread
- Butter
- 50 g/2 oz mature Cheddar cheese, grated
- A dash of Worcestershire sauce
- ½ crisp eating apple, thinly sliced
- 1-2 crisp lettuce leaves

Butter both slices of bread and cover one piece with the cheese. Sprinkle the cheese with the Worcestershire sauce and then add the apple slices and the lettuce. Top with the remaining slice of bread.

## WELSH RAREBIT

- 2 slices of bread
- Butter
- 25 g/1 oz mature Cheddar cheese, grated
- Salt and freshly ground black pepper
- Dollop of English mustard
- 1 dessertspoonful of beer or whisky
- 1-2 slices of tomato
- 1-2 crisp lettuce leaves

Butter both slices of bread. Mix the cheese with the salt and pepper, mustard and beer or whisky. Put the mixture into a small, non-stick pan and stir over a low heat until the cheese has melted and the mixture is smooth. Draw off the heat, cool and place on one slice of the bread. Top with the tomato and lettuce. Cover with the second slice of bread. This sandwich is also delicious toasted.

## AVOCADO

- 2 slices of bread
- Butter
- 1 tablespoonful avocado, peeled and stoned
- ½ hardboiled egg
- 1 heaped teaspoonful orange marmalade
- A few drops of lemon juice
- Pinch of nutmeg
- 1 dessertspoonful mayonnaise
- 1 teaspoonful chopped walnuts
- 1 dessertspoonful whipped cream

Butter both slices of bread. Mash the avocado with the egg, marmalade, lemon juice, nutmeg and mayonnaise. Stir in the walnuts and spread this mixture thickly on one slice of bread. Pile a generous helping of cream in the centre and top with the second slice of bread. This is also very good toasted.

## SPINACH, MUSHROOMS AND GARLIC

*2 slices of bread*
*Butter*
*4-5 spinach leaves, lightly cooked*
*1 tablespoonful chopped flat mushrooms*
*¼ clove of garlic, crushed*
*½ teaspoonful mayonnaise*
*½ tomato, sliced*
*1 teaspoonful sesame seeds*
*Salt and freshly ground black pepper*

*Butter both slices of bread. Chop the spinach and mushrooms together and mix with the garlic and mayonnaise. Top with the tomato and sesame seeds. Season to taste. Cover with the second slice of bread.*

## MUSHROOMS WITH SOURED CREAM

*2 slices of bread*
*Butter*
*1 tablespoonful flat mushrooms, sliced*
*¼ small onion, sliced*
*1 dessertspoonful soured cream*
*25 g/1 oz Cheddar cheese, grated*
*½ tomato, sliced*
*Salt and freshly ground black pepper*
*Large pinch of dried basil*
*1-2 crisp lettuce leaves*

*Butter both slices of bread. Lightly cook the mushrooms in a small amount of butter. Mix the mushrooms and onion in with the soured cream. Pile the mixture onto one slice of bread and top with the grated cheese and tomato. Season to taste and sprinkle basil on top. Cover with the lettuce leaves and the second slice of bread.*

## LEEKS, BEANS AND CARROTS

*2 slices of bread*
*Butter*
*1 dessertspoonful mayonnaise*
*1 small leek, thinly sliced*
*1 dessertspoonful tinned kidney beans*
*¼ clove garlic, crushed*
*¼ onion, finely chopped*
*1 dessertspoonful grated carrot*
*1 teaspoonful finely chopped pimento*
*½ hardboiled egg, sliced*
*1-2 crisp lettuce leaves*

*Butter both slices of bread. Mix the mayonnaise with the leek, kidney beans, garlic and onion and pile onto one slice of bread. Top with the grated carrot, pimento and egg. Cover with the lettuce leaves and the second slice of bread.*

## RUSSIAN SALAD

*2 slices of bread*
*Butter*
*½ crisp eating apple, thinly sliced*
*1 small stick of celery, diced*
*1 tablespoonful mayonnaise*
*Freshly ground black pepper*
*4-5 thin slices cooked beetroot*
*1-2 crisp lettuce leaves*

*Butter both slices of bread and add the apple slices to one piece of bread. Then stir together the celery, mayonnaise and pepper and spoon the mixture over the apple. Next add the beetroot and lettuce. Cover with the second slice of bread.*

## GINGER, WALNUTS AND DATES

*2 slices of bread*
*Butter*
*Peanut butter*
*1 dessertspoonful finely chopped fresh dates*
*1 dessertspoonful crushed walnuts*
*1 teaspoonful chopped ginger*
*A few drops of lemon juice*

*Butter both slices of bread. Spread the peanut butter generously on one slice, top with the dates, walnuts and ginger and squeeze lemon juice on top. Top with the second slice of bread.*

## MASHED BANANA AND GINGER JAM

*2 slices of bread*
*Butter*
*1 banana*
*A sprinkling of demerara sugar*
*A few drops of lemon juice*
*1 heaped teaspoonful whipped cream*
*1 dessertspoonful ginger jam*

*Butter both slices of bread. Mash the banana with the sugar and lemon juice. Spread one side of bread with this mixture and top with the whipped cream. Spread the second slice of bread with the ginger jam and cover the sandwich.*

# Gap Stoppers

*My goodness, this one was a difficult one to depict! 'Gap Stoppers,' I pondered to Johnny. 'Who would you think would be most interested in stopping a gap?' 'Teenagers,' he said, smartly (reliably ready with the swift solution). 'Teenagers are always starving. We'll round up some young athletes, swimmers or kids on a football field. And get a bakery somewhere to bake a specially long loaf, so that five or six of these kids could be biting into it, all at the same time. That'd look good, be a bit of fun.' 'Won't the filling fall out?' It needed one of us to be practical, not a role normally associated with me, I might add. 'Worth a try!' he beamed cheerfully, high on the act of creative thought. 'And since the picture can't be a horizontal, because of the shape of the page, we'll have them balanced on top of each other and turn it into a vertical. Have to be shot in the outdoors, on a sunny day, to give the right feeling of fresh air and youthful energy.' His eyes shone, he screwed them up tight, he opened them again and waved his arms. 'I can see it now,' he said, 'can't you, Moll?'*

*I stared back at him, stonily. I could see it, I do say that; but he must have proposed the admittedly bright plan at just the precise point in pre-menstrual tension (fellow-sufferers,* **you** *understand) when if I'd been offered the keys to the kingdom of Heaven, I'd have wanted to be sure first, before accepting, that some bastard hadn't changed the lock.*

*'I leave it to you, then.' I averted my eyes. 'Leave what?' He was astonished. 'Finding the five young jocks (jocks – Americanese for fitness freaks), the accommodating bakery, the filling that won't fall out, the outside ambience, and the sunny day. I leave it all for you to arrange.' Sourness writ large.*

*He burst out laughing. There are some days when Johnny's good humour is irrepressible. There are some days when mine is the same. We put it down to both being Aquarians. The fact that we've survived a working relationship for twenty-two years (I was pregnant with my second child when we first met) is simply that most of the time we share the same mood. This was not one of these days.*

*'Molly. You're a bit of a pain up the bum this morning, you know that?'*

*'John. A charming comment. Thank you very much. Any more where that came from?'*

*'A charming comment, but accurate would you say?'*

*'Accurate to a fault. Let's get back to Gap Stoppers. I'm thinking about lovers.'*

*He laughed again. 'Small wonder you can't concentrate on sandwiches. Let's leave your private life out of this.'*

*I sighed exaggeratedly. 'Lovers for Gap Stoppers. Lovers snatching a break in their marathon sessions for a spot of much-needed sustenance. We could have a blonde girl, but tanned. And a black guy with a beautiful body. We could chop their heads off – out of camera range, I mean, if they want to remain anonymous. And we could cut in close . . .'*

*'Close on what!?' Johnny's turn now for caution. 'Close on the sandwich for God's sake.' I was getting going. 'And we could have a great sandwich just to tie in for the colour. Pitta bread, humous, green and black olives. Subtle stuff, huh? We'll shoot it in the studio so that you can do some really moody lighting. I'll get in a load of black*

*and gold lamé fabric, for a touch of Eastern Promise. Turkish Delight. That's what we want. Be better than the sporty teenagers. Make more of a contrast with everything else that we've photographed.'*

*'The first piece of outright pornography, you mean?' His expression was pleasant enough. 'Should please the publishers. This is meant to be a book on sandwiches, remember. Young mums will have it on their recipe shelves in the kitchen, available for all the family, including impressionable children.'*

*'We'll be tasteful,' I insisted. 'I can be tasteful when I try. Don't be a Doubting Thomas, Johnny. Otherwise (crafty!) we'll go back to doing it your way, with you arranging it all.'*

*'It's your responsibility, then. I'll just stand behind the camera. This is one that you have to get together.'*

*It took me ten days to track down the two beautiful bodies in our snap! I was flabbergasted at how few people are prepared to remove their clothing for photography – in these days of permissiveness. After all, I was asking sun-worshippers, amongst others, who think nothing of scampering around starkers on a beach. But it was the fact of being pinned down for posterity in a sandwich book, I think that's what made them all say no! Then again, p'raps they didn't trust Johnny. Or me.*

## FRANKFURTERS AND COLESLAW

- 1/4 small white cabbage
- 1 carrot
- 1/4 onion
- 1/4 sweet green pepper
- 1 dessertspoonful mayonnaise
- Salt and freshly ground black pepper
- A few drops of lemon juice
- 1 roll or 1 15-cm/6-in piece of French stick
- Butter
- English or grain mustard
- 2 Frankfurters
- 2-3 thin slices of cucumber
- 1-2 crisp lettuce leaves

To make the coleslaw slice the cabbage, carrot, onion and green pepper thinly. Mix the vegetables with the mayonnaise, salt, pepper and lemon juice, making sure that the mayonnaise has covered all the ingredients thoroughly. Cut the roll or stick in half and spread each side with butter. Spread one side with mustard. Slice the Frankfurters lengthways and place on top of the mustard. Add a generous amount of coleslaw and top with the slices of cucumber and the crisp lettuce leaves. Cover with the second half of roll or stick.

## HOT DOG, CHEESE AND BACON

- 3 rashers streaky bacon
- 2 thin slices of bread
- Oil or melted butter
- 2-3 Frankfurters, split lengthways
- French mustard
- Tomato ketchup
- Salt and freshly ground black pepper
- 1 tablespoonful grated mature Cheddar cheese

Remove the rinds from the bacon, crisply cook and drain it. Brush one side of each slice of bread with oil or butter. Arrange the Frankfurters on the dry side of one slice of bread, spread mustard and tomato ketchup on top and then add the bacon rashers. Add the seasoning and sprinkle on the Cheddar cheese. Cover with the remaining slice of bread, oiled or buttered side up. Cook under the grill or in a preheated oven, 200°C, 400°F, Gas Mark 6, until crisp.

## HAMBURGER IN SESAME SEED ROLL

- 1 sesame seed roll
- Butter
- 100 g/ 1/4 lb good minced beef
- Pinch of mixed herbs
- 1/4 teaspoonful tomato ketchup
- Salt and freshly ground black pepper
- 1/4 teaspoonful Worcestershire sauce
- 1/4 medium-sized onion, thinly sliced
- 1/2 tomato, sliced
- 1-2 crisp lettuce leaves
- Mustard of your choice

Cut the roll in half and butter both halves. Mix together the mince, herbs, ketchup, seasoning and Worcestershire sauce. Bind into a flattish, roundish ball and grill to your taste – rare, medium or well done. Leave to cool and then place on one half of the roll. Top with the onion, tomato and lettuce. Spread the second side of the roll with the mustard and cover. This is also very good toasted but remember to toast lightly the inside of the roll before adding the filling so that the bread does not become soggy.

## CORNED BEEF AND HORSERADISH SAUCE

- 1 roll or 2 slices of bread
- Butter
- 2 slices corned beef
- 1/2 tomato, sliced
- 1-2 crisp lettuce leaves
- 1 heaped teaspoonful horseradish sauce

Butter both halves of the roll or slices of bread. Place the corned beef on one half of roll or on one slice of bread. Cover with the tomato and lettuce. Spread the horseradish sauce on the second slice of bread or half of roll and cover the sandwich. This is good toasted.

## CORNED BEEF HASH

- 1 level dessertspoonful onion, chopped
- 2 slices of bread
- Oil or melted butter
- 1 heaped dessertspoonful boiled potato
- 50 g/2 oz crumbled corned beef
- 1 dessertspoonful tomato chutney
- Salt and freshly ground black pepper

Fry the onion lightly. Brush oil or butter on the two slices of bread. Break up the potato with a small fork. Mix together the corned beef, potato and onion and bind with the tomato chutney. Spread the mixture evenly over the dry surface of one slice of bread, add the seasoning and cover with the second slice of bread, oiled or buttered side up. Cook in a preheated oven, 200°C, 400°F, Gas Mark 6, or under the grill until crisp.

## HAM, CHEESE AND PICKLE SALAD

- 2 slices of bread or
- 1 15-cm/6-in piece of French stick
- Butter
- English mustard
- 2 slices of ham
- 2 slices mature Cheddar cheese
- ½ tomato, sliced
- ¼ cucumber, thinly sliced
- 1-2 crisp lettuce leaves
- 1 teaspoonful mayonnaise
- 1 dessertspoonful pickle
- Salt and freshly ground black pepper

Spread both sliced of bread or sides of French stick with butter. Spread mustard thinly on the first slice of bread or stick. Cover with the ham, cheese, tomato, cucumber and lettuce. Spread mayonnaise and pickle on the second slice of bread or roll and cover to make a sandwich.

## CHICKEN SALAD

- 1 roll or 2 slices of bread
- Butter
- 2 slices cooked cold chicken
- Salt and freshly ground black pepper
- Chicken seasoning
- ¾ cucumber, thinly sliced
- ¼ tomato, sliced
- 1-2 crisp lettuce leaves
- Mayonnaise

Butter both halves of roll or both slices of bread. Place the chicken on one half or slice and season with salt, pepper and a sprinkling of chicken seasoning. Top with the cucumber, tomato and lettuce. Spread mayonnaise on the second half or slice and cover the sandwich.

## CHICKEN LIVERS AND BACON

- 3-4 chicken livers
- 1 rasher streaky bacon
- 2 thin slices of bread
- Butter
- 1/4 onion, finely sliced and cooked
- Pinch of mixed herbs
- Salt and freshly ground black pepper
- 1 heaped teaspoonful tomato ketchup
- 1/2 tomato, sliced
- 1-2 crisp lettuce leaves
- French mustard

*Cook the chicken livers in a small amount of butter until the outsides have changed colour and the insides are still slightly pink. Be careful not to overcook them. Chop them into small pieces. Remove the rinds from the bacon, crisply cook and dice it. Butter both slices of bread. Mix together the chicken livers, bacon, onion, herbs, salt, pepper and ketchup. If you prefer a purée, put these ingredients into a blender and process for a few seconds.*

*Spread this mixture onto the first slice of bread and top with the tomato and lettuce. Spread the second slice of bread with mustard and cover the sandwich. This is also very good toasted.*

## TURKEY, BACON AND GRUYERE

- 25 g/1 oz rashers back bacon
- 1 piece of pitta bread
- Butter
- English mustard to taste
- Mayonnaise
- 1-2 1-cm/1/4-in slices of cooked turkey
- 1-2 slices ham
- 1-2 slices Gruyère cheese
- 1 dessertspoonful potato salad
- 3 slices tomato
- Salt and freshly ground black pepper
- 2-3 crisp lettuce leaves

*Remove the rinds from the bacon and lightly cook it. Make a lengthways incision on one of the flat sides of the piece of pitta bread and open it out. Butter the inside on both sides and spread with mustard and mayonnaise to taste. Carefully place the bacon, turkey, ham and cheese in decks inside. Cover with the potato salad and tomato slices and season to taste. Cover with the lettuce and close the sandwich.*

# HUMOUS IN PITTA BREAD

*50 g/2 oz humous*
*A few drops of lemon juice*
*¼ teaspoonful oil*
*1 teaspoonful chopped onion*
*1 piece of pitta bread, lightly grilled*
*3 each black and green olives, stoned*
*Italian parsley for garnishing*

*Mix the humous with the lemon juice, oil and onion. Cut the pitta bread in half lengthways but not right through. Spoon the humous mixture into the bread and decorate with the olives and parsley. This is also very good with lettuce leaves added on top of the humous.*

# SALMON FISH CAKES

*8 rolls*
*450 g/1 lb tinned pink salmon, drained*
*450 g/1 lb potatoes, boiled and mashed*
*1 tablespoonful finely chopped parsley*
*1 tablespoonful tomato ketchup*
*A few drops of lemon juice*
*Salt and freshly ground black pepper*
*2 small eggs*
*Breadcrumbs*
*100g/¼ lb butter plus 2 tablespoons oil*
*4 tomatoes, sliced*
*16 crisp lettuce leaves*

*This makes enough for eight rolls, one fish cake each. Cut the rolls in half and butter the insides on both sides. In a bowl mix the drained salmon with the mashed potato, parsley, tomato ketchup and lemon juice. Season to taste and make sure that the ingredients are really well mixed together. Beat the eggs lightly and add half the mixture to the bowl in order to bind the salmon and potato.*

*Turn the salmon mixture onto a floured board and form into round cakes, making eight in all. Dip the cakes into the remaining egg mixture and coat them evenly all over. Then dip them into the breadcrumbs and coat evenly. Pat on firmly, making sure that the cakes keep their shape.*

*Heat the oil and butter in a frying pan, add the fish cakes and fry them until they are golden brown. Place a hot fish cake into each buttered roll, together with sliced tomato and lettuce. Alternatively, cool the fish cakes and eat them with a roll or bread separately.*

## GARLIC SHRIMPS WITH BACON AND CHEESE

- 1 rasher streaky bacon
- 2 thin slices of bread
- Butter
- 1 heaped dessertspoonful shrimps, cooked
- 1 small clove garlic, crushed
- 1 heaped tablespoonful mayonnaise
- 1 tablespoonful cream cheese
- 2-3 thin slices cucumber
- Salt and freshly ground black pepper
- 2-3 crisp lettuce leaves

Remove the rinds from the bacon, crisply cook and crumble it. Butter both slices of the bread. Peel the shrimps if necessary and mix them with the bacon and garlic and add to the mayonnaise. Spread one slice of the bread with the cream cheese and top with the shrimp and garlic mixture. Top with the cucumber slices and season to taste. Cover with the lettuce and the second slice of bread. This is also very good toasted.

## GRILLED COD'S ROE AND BACON

- 25 g/1 oz cod's roe
- 3 rashers streaky bacon
- 2 thin slices of bread
- Oil or melted butter
- A few drops of lemon juice
- A few drops of Worcestershire sauce
- Pinch of chopped parsley

Cook the cod's roe in a small amount of butter for 2-3 minutes. Remove the rinds from the bacon, crisply cook and drain it. Brush one side of each slice of bread with oil or butter. Spread the cod's roe on the dry surface of one slice and sprinkle with lemon juice and Worcestershire sauce. Sprinkle the parsley on top. Then arrange the rashers of bacon on top of the roes and add the second slice of bread, oiled or buttered side up. Cook under the grill or in a preheated oven, 200°C, 400°F, Gas Mark 6, until crisp.

# Tea at the Ritz

*We took Dame Edna Everage for tea at the Ritz. Well, it was obvious, wasn't it? Johnny rang Barry Humphries first to check that it could be arranged, since Barrie is Dame Edna's social secretary and seems to know where she's going to be just about every single moment of the day. It's astounding how closely in touch those two are. The same rapport as Charlie McCarthy had with Edgar Bergen, or Emu with what's-'is-name.*

*Dame Edna was late. But that's what you expect from superstars and Johnny had warned that she would be, he knows because he photographs Dame Edna all the time. She likes him best of the photographers because he understands about lighting glamorous ladies – dare I say it – of a certain age. He knows how to bring out the best in them.*

*The rest of us sat around getting edgy while we waited, especially the sweet and dauntingly pretty Publicity Person of the Ritz. We'd promised her that we'd be all through with the pictures before the public started queuing for their tea-time tables proper. And indeed they had started to line up (tea at the Ritz is* **very** *popular, you have to be on time to be sure of a table), then miraculously Dame Edna arrived!*

*I say 'miraculously' because that was how it seemed. As if a miracle had occurred. The atmosphere altered. The heavens opened. A celestial choir started singing out of nowhere. The crowds parted as Her Magnificence swept into view. We were truly in the presence of a World Superstar.*

*Now I've seen stars in my time, you might even call them superstars (using a small 's' instead of a large). I've sat in the same restaurant, the famous Sardi's in New York, with Elizabeth Taylor at the* **start** *of her romance with Richard Burton! And all eyes were on them, including mine, I admit. But the occasion was blighted, though I'm prepared to state now that her beauty was blinding, for me she'd damaged her image.* ***There was dandruff all over her collar!***

*The same as when I saw Ursula Andress at the traffic lights in a taxi alongside mine. She was crying and all her mascara had run down her cheeks right into her mouth. You'd have thought they would have kitted her out with the waterproof sort, coming from Hollywood. Now I make sure never to weep when I'm waiting for lights to change in the street. Either that or go out without make-up, which I don't think that any girl should risk, however few fans she may have.*

*Dame Edna certainly hadn't held back on her 'maquillage'. Porcelain perfection, not an open pore in sight. She'd have put even Barbara Cartland in the shade. And her perfume – I don't know what it was – how would one have dared ask? But the costly display of flowers there in the foyer of the Ritz Hotel, they hung their petalled heads in shame. Quite right too.*

*She glided forward, graciously accepting our obsequious greeting and the proffered chair at the prime positioned table in the tea-room. Seeming unaware, in the royal tradition, of the immediate chaos occurring in her wake, as dignified matrons and men of good standing chucked breeding to the birds in a bid for the next tables to hers.*

*The head waiter arrived with a flourish to present a silver salver of sandwiches, garnished with appropriate sprays of gladiolas (we all know that gladdies are Dame*

*Edna's favourite 'fleurs'). She took a kittenishly long time choosing just which sandwiches she'd like (cucumber or smoked salmon – the cukes, in wafer-slim slivers being the 'spécialité de la maison'). But her fans were entranced, finding in her performance shades of Scarlett O'Hara from 'Gone With The Wind'.*

*They held their breath as she daintily took her first delicate bite. We all did, because Johnny had warned what would happen if she found the Ritz sandwiches to her liking. He said that she'd probably want to share them with everyone, toss them at her adoring public in the way that she tosses her gladdies . . .*

*Which she started to do. But the pretty Publicity Person of the Ritz stepped up, just in the nick of time. The Superstar departed, shrugging sweetly, with her famous smile. The celestial choir receded. It was back to normal tea at the Ritz.*

## CUCUMBER

- 2 thin slices of brown bread
- Butter
- 5-6 wafer-thin slices cucumber
- 1-2 crisp lettuce leaves
- Salt and freshly ground black pepper
- Mayonnaise

Butter the bread before cutting the slices from the loaf, this makes thinner and better slices. Place the cucumber on one slice of bread and cover with the lettuce. Season to taste. Spread mayonnaise thinly on the second slice and cover the sandwich. Remove the crusts and cut into quarters.

## SAVOURY SARDINE AND MUSHROOM

- 3-4 flat mushrooms, finely chopped
- 2 thin slices of brown bread
- Butter
- 2-3 sardines in oil, well drained
- 1 hardboiled egg, chopped
- 1 small onion, finely chopped and fried
- A dash of Worcestershire sauce
- Mayonnaise

Fry the mushrooms gently in a small amount of butter. Butter both slices of bread. Mash the sardines with the hardboiled egg and the onion. Spread the mixture on one slice of bread and sprinkle with Worcestershire sauce. Arrange the mushrooms on top. Cover the second slice of bread with a layer of mayonnaise and close the sandwich. Remove the crusts and cut into quarters.

## ANCHOVY FILLETS AND OLIVES

*2 thin slices of brown bread*
*Butter*
*3-4 anchovy fillets in oil, well drained*
*3-4 green olives*
*1 teaspoonful mayonnaise*
*Freshly ground black pepper*

*Butter both slices of bread. Place the anchovy fillets on one slice. Stone the olives and finely chop them. Mix them with the mayonnaise and add the pepper. Spread this mixture over the anchovy fillets and top with the second slice of bread. Remove the crusts and cut into quarters.*

## SMOKED SALMON

*2 thin slices of brown bread*
*Butter*
*2 slices of smoked salmon*
*Pinch of cayenne pepper*
*A few drops of lemon juice*
*3-4 wafer-thin slices cucumber*
*2-3 crisp lettuce leaves*

*Butter both slices of bread. Place the salmon on one slice and sprinkle with cayenne pepper and lemon juice. Cover with the cucumber and lettuce and close the sandwich. Remove the crusts and cut into quarters.*

## GENTLEMAN'S RELISH WITH MUSHROOMS

*2 thin slices of brown bread*
*Butter*
*1 teaspoonful Gentleman's Relish*
*1 dessertspoonful chopped flat mushrooms, fried*
*1 teaspoonful mayonnaise*

*Butter both slices of bread. Spread both slices with a thin smear of Gentleman's Relish. Bind the mushrooms with the mayonnaise and spread the mixture on one of the slices of bread. Cover with the second slice, remove the crusts and cut into quarters.*

## CORNISH CREAM TEA

*1 scone or roll*
*Cornish butter*
*Thick strawberry jam*
*Cornish clotted cream*

*Cut the scone or roll in half and butter generously on both halves. Fill with strawberry jam and clotted cream.*

# Twelfth August

Some mortals are sort of special. They exude an air of breeding which transforms them into rarefied beauties, like certain species in the animal kingdom. Flamingos, for instance. And storks. And swans. Greta Garbo. Grace Kelly. Vivien Leigh. And closer to home, 'cos I happen to know them both, the actress Sian Phillips and Barbara Hulanicki (of Biba fame).

I thought of these two friends when Topsy presented me with the chapter heading, Twelfth of August. I was frankly mystified because I didn't know what the hell it meant. 'What happens on the Twelfth of August?' I asked. 'Oh, come on, Moll. You know very well.' But I honestly didn't. It was the wrong time for Guy Fawkes. Liberace hadn't a wedding anniversary. Max Miller and Monroe didn't die on that day (or p'haps they did). It wasn't Christmas, or Easter, or American Independence. . . .

'Tell me, Topsy dear. Put me out of my ignorance.'

'It's the day the shooting starts.'

She didn't mean people, though that can happen at any time, with the way the world is at the moment. I think she said grouse. Or did she say pheasant (what **is** the difference – they both fly don't they?). Somehow I cottoned on to it being something to do with ducks, which was why she and everyone else was probably so mystified when I outlined my proposal for the Twelfth of August photograph.

'What we need is a really tacky suburban wallpaper, with those plaster flying ducks – like Hilda Ogden has on her mural in "Coronation Street". Got it?'

Johnny agreed with me wholeheartedly. We saw eye to bloodshot eye on this one right from the start. 'But Moll, why?' Topsy mildly enquired. 'Because,' I explained, 'if we pose someone like Barbara or Sian, sophisticated and classy, against the crappiness of the background we'll have the best of both worlds. It's called camping the whole thing up.' 'But wouldn't it just be simpler to shoot the real thing out on a moor, Moll?' 'Much simpler!' Johnny answered on behalf of us both. 'But we're not drawn to do anything unless there are insurmountable problems. Right, Moll?' 'Sure thing, Johnny!'

The problems presented themselves without any trouble, no trying on our part. Barbara (I'd forgotten) is pathologically camera-shy and simply refuses **ever** to sit for photographs. Sian, as it turned out, was unavailable though enthusiastic. She was filming over in Ireland. 'What about Garbo, then?' I suggested to Johnny. 'I'm sure your charms could work the oracle there if you tried, luv.' He blew an extremely rude raspberry in reply. Really helpful.

Back to Barbara and the most insidious pressure on my part. 'We could talk about your novel (Barbara is struggling with her first). I might be able to pass you a few tips' (I'm on my twelfth and in possession of various helpful hints passed on from other novelist pals). Our friendship goes back almost as long as Johnny's and mine. After my first divorce, when I found it unbearable to paint in the solitude on my studio, I actually used to make hats and handbags for the very first Biba shop. Barbara tells me that when Fitz (her hunky husband) saw me coming to collect my cash, he'd run out of the back door to escape. But such a ruse never worked with me, no way! I'd sit in the 'soigné' shop with my Sarah and Sophie and several of their small schoolfriends, passing round sticky sweets, allowing them complete freedom to scuffle through the stock. The friendship continued, on a proper *business basis. Indeed, it flourished; I think my tactics must have impressed the businessman in Fitz. I was the only one to get paid at the* **precise** *point of handing over the merchandising in the right hand, whilst receiving the money in the left!*

*When my very first novel 'Love All' was published, Barbara and Fitz threw a launching party for me at Biba, which by then was the vast emporium on Ken. High Street. 'What will you be wearing?' Barbara rang up to ask. 'Oh, red and white. That's all we're wearing in our house at the moment. Our latest thing.'*

*I arrived to find that the flabbergasting banquet prepared in the Biba Rainbow Room consisted of food that was solely scarlet and white! Red sausages and white mash, scarlet shrimps and white rice, ruby jelly and white ice cream, bright strawberries and white cream. And the whole place decked out in red and white roses. Oh, she's got some* **style**, *has Barbara! And generosity. She posed for this photo. Got herself dressed up to look the part, though one detail perplexed her. No damask handkerchief on which to hold the sandwich! The fault of* **this** *slovenly, lesser mortal, I fear . . .*

## DUCK WITH SWEET AND SOUR SAUCE

- 2 slices of bread
- Butter
- 2 thick slices of roast duck
- A sprinkling of sweet and sour sauce
- 3-4 flat mushrooms, cooked
- Salt and freshly ground black pepper
- 2-3 thin slices of tomato
- 1-2 crisp lettuce leaves

Butter both slices of bread. Arrange the slices of duck on one slice of bread and cover with a sprinkling of sweet and sour sauce. Add the mushrooms, seasoning, tomato and lettuce. Top with the second slice of bread.

## TURKEY AND BLUE CHEESE

- 2-3 rashers streaky bacon
- 2 slices of bread
- Butter
- Mayonnaise
- 1-2 thick slices of cooked turkey breast
- 1 dessertspoonful Blue cheese, crumbled
- 3-4 slices of avocado, peeled
- A few drops of lemon juice
- Salt and freshly ground black pepper
- 1-2 crisp lettuce leaves

Remove the rinds from the bacon, crisply cook and dice it. Butter both sides of bread. Spread one slice generously with mayonnaise and cover with the turkey, bacon, cheese and avocado. Sprinkle the avocado with lemon juice, season to taste and cover with the lettuce leaves. Top with the second slice of bread. This is also very good toasted.

## TURKEY AND AVOCADO

- 2 slices of bread
- Butter
- 1-2 slices of cooked turkey breast
- 1/4 avocado, peeled and mashed
- 1 teaspoonful finely grated onion
- A few drops of lemon juice
- Salt and freshly ground black pepper
- 2-3 slices cucumber
- 1-2 crisp lettuce leaves

Butter both slices of bread. Place the turkey on one slice. Then mix the mashed avocado together with the onion and lemon juice. Pile this mixture onto the turkey and season to taste. Cover with the cucumber and lettuce leaves. Top with the second slice of bread.

## CHICKEN AND CHEDDAR

- 1-2 flat mushrooms
- 2 thin slices of brown bread or
- 1 15-cm/6-in piece of French stick
- Butter
- French mustard
- 1 dessertspoonful cooked chicken
- Salt and freshly ground black pepper
- 1 dessertspoonful Cheddar cheese, grated
- 1/4 onion, thinly sliced
- 1/4 pimento, thinly sliced
- 1-2 crisp lettuce leaves
- Mayonnaise

Thinly slice the mushrooms and cook gently in a small amount of butter. Spread both halves of the stick or the slices of bread with butter. Spread French mustard on one half of the stick or on one piece of bread. Coarsely chop the cooked chicken. Top one half with the chicken, seasoning, cheese, onion, pimento, mushrooms and lettuce. Spread the second piece of bread with mayonnaise and cover the sandwich.

## PORK AND APPLE SAUCE

- 2 slices of bread
- Butter
- 1-2 slices of roast pork
- 1 heaped teaspoonful apple sauce
- Salt and freshly ground black pepper
- 2-3 slices of cucumber
- 1-2 crisp lettuce leaves
- A scraping of mayonnaise
- A scraping of English mustard

Butter both slices of bread. Place the pork on one slice and top with the apple sauce, salt, pepper, cucumber slices and lettuce. Spread the second slice of bread with a scraping of mayonnaise and mustard and cover the sandwich.

## HAM WITH PEARS

- 2 slices of bread
- Butter
- Mayonnaise
- 1-2 slices of lean ham
- ½ small, firm pear, peeled and cored
- A sprinkling of lemon juice
- 2 small spring onions, finely chopped
- A sprinkling of cress
- 1-2 crisp lettuce leaves
- 25 g/1 oz cream cheese

Butter both slices of bread. Spread mayonnaise generously on one slice of bread and cover with the ham. Slice the pear thinly and sprinkle all over with lemon juice. Place the slices of pear on top of the ham, cover with the spring onions, cress and lettuce leaves. Spread the cream cheese on the second slice of bread and cover the sandwich.

## HAM WITH CHICKEN LIVERS

- Chicken liver from 1 chicken
- 2 slices of bread
- Butter
- 1 tablespoonful minced ham
- ¼ small onion, finely chopped
- A dash of Worcestershire sauce
- A generous dash of tomato ketchup
- Salt and freshly ground black pepper
- 1 hardboiled egg, sliced
- ¼ tomato, sliced
- 1-2 sprigs of watercress
- Mayonnaise

Cook the chicken liver in a small amount of butter and mince finely. Butter both slices of bread. Mix the minced ham and chicken liver together with the onion, Worcestershire sauce, tomato ketchup and seasoning. Spread this mixture on one slice of bread and top with the sliced egg, tomato and watercress. Spread the second slice of bread with mayonnaise and close the sandwich.

## GAMMON AND PINEAPPLE

- 2 slices of bread or one roll
- Butter
- A scraping of English mustard
- 1 large, thick slice of cooked gammon
- 1 thick pineapple ring, fresh or tinned
- 1-2 crisp lettuce leaves
- Mayonnaise

Butter both slices of bread or halves of roll. If using tinned pineapple, drain well. Spread one piece of bread or half of roll with mustard, then place the gammon, pineapple and lettuce leaves on top. Spread the second slice or half with mayonnaise and cover the sandwich.

## BACON WITH PRUNES

- 3-4 rashers streaky bacon
- 2 slices of granary bread
- Butter
- English mustard
- 2-3 prunes, stones removed and halved
- 2-3 slices of tomato
- 1 large sprig of watercress
- 1-2 crisp lettuce leaves
- Freshly ground black pepper
- Mayonnaise

Remove the rinds from the bacon and cook it crisply. Butter both slices of bread and spread mustard on one slice. Then lay the bacon on top, cover with the prunes and tomato. Season to taste. Add the watercress and lettuce leaves. Spread mayonnaise on the second slice of bread and top the sandwich.

## SPINACH, BACON AND BEANS

- 2 slices of bread
- Butter
- 2-3 rashers streaky bacon
- 1 heaped tablespoonful cooked spinach
- 1 dessertspoonful cooked young broad beans
- 1 teaspoonful dried marjoram and basil
- 1 small clove of garlic, crushed
- Salt and freshly ground black pepper
- 1-2 crisp lettuce leaves
- Mayonnaise

Remove the rinds from the bacon and cook it crisply. Butter both slices of bread. Chop the spinach roughly. Spread the spinach thickly on one slice and top with the streaky bacon and broad beans. Sprinkle with the herbs, garlic, salt and pepper. Add the lettuce on top. Spread the second slice of bread with mayonnaise and close the sandwich. This is also very good toasted.

## TONGUE AND SPINACH

- 2 slices of bread
- Butter
- 1-2 slices cooked lamb's tongue
- 1 tablespoonful cooked spinach, drained
- ¼ clove of garlic, crushed
- Salt and freshly ground black pepper
- ¼ tomato, sliced
- Mayonnaise

Butter both slices of bread. Place the tongue on one slice. Mix the spinach with the garlic and season to taste. Pile this mixture on top of the tongue. Cover with the tomato. Spread the second slice of bread with mayonnaise and cover the sandwich.

## FRANKFURTERS AND CHEESE

- 2 slices of bread
- Butter
- 2 Frankfurters, cut in half lengthways
- 1 dessertspoonful grated mature Cheddar cheese
- 2-3 onion rings
- 1 teaspoonful finely chopped peppers
- 1-2 crisp lettuce leaves
- Mayonnaise
- French mustard

Butter both slices of bread. Place the Frankfurters on one slice and top with the cheese, onion rings, peppers and lettuce leaves. Spread the second slice of bread with mayonnaise and French mustard and close the sandwich.

## MACKEREL AND CHEESE WITH BACON

- 1 rasher back bacon
- 2 slices of bread
- Butter
- 1 tablespoonful smoked mackerel
- 1 small teaspoonful double cream
- Salt and freshly ground black pepper
- 1 hardboiled egg, sliced
- 1 dessertspoonful Cheddar cheese, grated
- ½ tomato, sliced
- 1-2 crisp lettuce leaves

Remove the rinds from the bacon and cook it crisply. Butter both slices of bread. Flake the fish, removing all bones, and mix it with the cream. Season to taste. Pile this mixture onto one slice of bread and top with the bacon, egg, cheese, tomato and lettuce leaves. Cover with the second slice of bread.

## SALMON TROUT WITH HOLLANDAISE

- 2 thin slices of brown bread
- Butter
- 1 tablespoonful salmon trout, cooked
- 1 dessertspoonful hollandaise sauce
- A sprinkling of dill
- Salt and freshly ground black pepper
- 2-3 slices cucumber, wafer-thin
- 1-2 crisp lettuce leaves

Butter both slices of bread. Skin the salmon trout and mix it with the hollandaise. If you have no hollandaise, you can always use mayonnaise. Sprinkle a little dill with salt and pepper over the mixture. Heap this mixture onto one slice of bread and cover with the cucumber and lettuce leaves. Top with the second slice of bread.

## CRAB AND PARMESAN CHEESE

- 2 slices of bread
- Butter
- 1 tablespoonful crabmeat, fresh or frozen
- A pinch of cayenne pepper
- Dash of brandy
- ½ teaspoonful double cream
- 1 teaspoonful Parmesan cheese
- 2-3 slices of cucumber
- 2-3 crisp lettuce leaves

Butter both slices of bread. If using frozen crabmeat, allow it to thaw first. Mix the crab with cayenne pepper, brandy and cream. Be careful not to overdo the cream as it could become soggy. Pile the mixture onto one slice of bread, sprinkle with the cheese, top with the cucumber and lettuce and the second slice of bread.

## CRABMEAT AND MUSHROOMS

- 1 tablespoonful fresh or frozen crabmeat
- 2 slices of brown bread
- Butter
- 1-2 flat mushrooms, very finely chopped
- 1 teaspoonful Parmesan cheese
- 1 dessertspoonful mayonnaise
- Pinch of parsley, rosemary, sage and thyme
- Salt and freshly ground black pepper
- A sprinkling of crushed almonds
- 1-2 crisp lettuce leaves

If the crabmeat is frozen, thaw and drain it. Butter both slices of bread. Combine the crabmeat, mushrooms, cheese and mayonnaise and all the seasonings together and spread on the first slice of bread. Sprinkle with almonds, cover with the lettuce and close the sandwich. Remove the crusts and cut into quarters.

## CREAMED TUNA AND ANCHOVY

- 2 slices of bread
- Butter
- 1 tablespoonful tuna fish in brine, well drained
- 1 dessertspoonful mayonnaise
- ¼ teaspoonful anchovy essence or to taste
- A pinch of cayenne pepper
- Freshly ground black pepper
- ½ teaspoonful finely chopped onion
- ½ tomato, sliced
- 1-2 crisp lettuce leaves

Butter both slices of bread. Mash the tuna fish with the mayonnaise, anchovy essence, cayenne and black pepper. Add the chopped onion. Pile this mixture onto one slice of bread and top with the tomato and lettuce. Cover with the second slice of bread.

# Director's Working Lunch

*'Who do we know who's a director, Johnny?'*

*'Which world? Theatrical? Film? You want Polanski? Ken Rissole? Fellini-ini?'*

*Johnny was skittish. We'd both just polished off a 'Dusty Road'* ***each*** *in our favourite tea-shop, Richoux. 'Dusty Roads' come in pint-size portions consisting of glorious butterscotch syrup bases, alternating with layers of ice-cream and whipped cream. Topped off with a dusting of overrich dark chocolate. You feel decidedly sick when, and if, you ever get to the end. And light-headed. The weighty heaviness appears on the hips some twenty-four hours later.*

*I giggled. 'Let's be sensible. This is our very last photo. We must make it marvellous. But who do we know who looks affluent enough to be chairman of the board?'*

*'A friend? No-one.'*

*'No. That's what I thought. We don't have any friends like that, do we? Well, let's start again. Who do we know who looks* ***least*** *like the chairman of the board?'*

*The thought came to us simultaneously. It does do that sometimes. 'Dud!' 'Dudley Sutton!' 'You ask him,' I said. 'No. You.' I did ask him. He said OK. Just as a favour for old mates. When he arrived in his suit I nearly walked past him. In fact, where we shot the photograph in The Chelsea Art Club, a club all three of us belong to, hardly anybody did recognize Dudley.*

*It wasn't just the suit, or the groomed Jermyn Street-style hairdo. It was the total demeanour. The affable expansiveness. The capitalist confidence. The fat cat, cock-of-the-walk, the king-of-the-castle. The* ***smoothie****. I couldn't get over the silky sensuality.* ***Couldn't****. I started simpering, I did. Hoping he'd notice me and say something nice, any small crumb would have done. But all I got was a steady and decidedly insolent stare of top-to-toe appraisal. Then a chilling sneer of chiselled lips and slightly raised left eyebrow. He made me feel like some common slut. I really had to tell him that. After all I've known Dud almost since the year dot. I slavishly followed his career even before I became his friend, and can recall every one of his memorable performances. Who could forget his Mr Sloane? Dudley Sutton was the originator of that role (in Joe Orton's 'Entertaining Mr Sloane') and for most people's money the most menacing.*

*'I don't know who you think you are,' I challenged him, wriggling the while, 'looking at me like that. You make me feel like some common slut.' There – it was out.*

*'Shut* ***up****, you strumpet!'*

*I gaped back at him. I understand that Clothes Maketh the Man, and that Dudley is about the most consummate actor I know, and this was called 'getting into character', but I could see that even Johnny was beginning to react. He was positively* ***genuflecting*** *– a touch of the Uriah Heeps.*

*'It's to be hoped that when we finish this photo you'll return to being your normal Peter Pan self, Dudley.' I coaxed a cosy chumminess into my tones.*

*'Kindly address me in a more formal fashion, Madam.' Cigar smoke muffled the menace (Dudley hasn't smoked for I don't know how many years!). I kept mum until it was over.*

*The thing that was fascinating was how mesmerizing he was. The staff from the kitchen came out to stand and watch. Early customers for the Club lunch delayed their orders to watch also. It's the appearance of affluence that's doing it, I thought. The power. That's the aphrodisiac. You'd only have to remember an ugly little runt like Onassis, who had his choice of the world's most beautiful women. Power.*

*The next time we met, Dudley and I, it was for a nice cup of tea together. He was back to normal. Sloppy sneakers. Dylan Thomas hair. Baggy suit from Johnson and Johnson. T-shirt sporting some anarchy or other.*

*'Nice to be back with Puck, Dud,' I said. 'Not that I didn't find the Jimmy Goldsmith act oddly attractive.'*

*'Sir James Goldsmith, woman, if you don't mind.' He'd put on the plummy voice again.*

*'Don't do that, Dud.' I pleaded. 'Don't. I find it gives me a terrible and rather wonderful 'frisson'.' True. And tragic to think of all those wasted years, past, when I could have devoted myself to being a rich man's darling. A piece on the side, for the chairman of the board.*

## CHILLI-CON-CARNE AND AVOCADO

- *2 slices of bread or 1 roll*
- *Butter*
- *1 tablespoonful leftover chilli-con-carne*
- *1 heaped teaspoonful avocado, mashed*
- *2-3 slices finely chopped onion*
- *1-2 crisp lettuce leaves*

*Butter both slices of bread or halves of roll. Spread one slice or half with chilli-con-carne and top with the avocado, onion and lettuce. Cover with the second slice of bread or half of roll.*

## LAMB WITH SPINACH AND PEACH CHUTNEY

- *2 slices of bread*
- *Butter*
- *2-3 thin slices of roast lamb*
- *Salt and freshly ground black pepper*
- *1 dessertspoonful peach chutney*
- *3-4 fresh spinach leaves, washed*
- *Mayonnaise*

*Butter both slices of bread. Place the lamb on one slice and season to taste. Cover with the peach chutney and spinach leaves. Spread mayonnaise thinly on the second slice of bread and close the sandwich.*

## PORK AND RED CABBAGE

- 2 slices of bread
- Butter
- 1-2 thick slices of roast pork
- 1 dessertspoonful pickled red cabbage
- 2-3 slices tart eating apple, peeled
- Salt and freshly ground black pepper
- 1-2 crisp lettuce leaves
- Mayonnaise

Butter both slices of bread. Place the pork on one slice and top with the cabbage and apple. Season to taste and add the lettuce. Spread the second slice of bread with mayonnaise and close the sandwich.

## PORK AND PICKLED ONION

- 2 slices of bread
- Butter
- 50 g/2 oz thinly cut roast pork
- Apple sauce
- 1 dessertspoonful finely sliced pickled onion
- 4-5 thin slices cucumber
- 1-2 crisp lettuce leaves
- Mayonnaise

Butter both slices of bread. Place the pork on one slice and spread with a thin layer of apple sauce. Sprinkle the pickled onion on top, then add the cucumber and lettuce leaves. Spread mayonnaise on the second slice and cover the sandwich.

## BACON WITH MUSHROOMS

- 2 rashers streaky bacon
- 2 slices of bread or 1 roll
- Butter
- English or grain mustard
- 1-2 flat mushrooms, cooked
- 1-2 slices of tomato
- 1 sprig of watercress
- 1-2 crisp lettuce leaves
- Mayonnaise

Remove the rinds from the bacon and cook it crisply. Drain well. Butter both slices of bread or halves of roll. Spread one slice or half of roll with mustard and add the bacon, mushrooms, tomato, watercress and lettuce leaves. Spread the second slice or half of bread with mayonnaise and close the sandwich.

## GAMMON WITH POTATO SALAD AND HONEY

- 2 slices of bread or 1 roll
- Butter
- 1 teaspoonful clear honey
- 1 thick slice of cooked gammon
- 1 dessertspoonful potato salad
- 1-2 crisp lettuce leaves
- Freshly ground black pepper

*Butter both slices of bread or halves of roll. Spread one slice with honey and cover with the gammon, potato salad and lettuce leaves. Season with pepper. Spread mustard on the second slice of bread or half of roll and cover the sandwich.*

## CUMBERLAND SAUSAGES WITH TOMATO

- 2 slices of bread or 1 roll
- Butter
- Grain mustard
- 2 Cumberland sausages, cooked and halved
- 2-3 slices of tomato
- 1-2 crisp lettuce leaves
- Mayonnaise

*Butter both slices of bread or halves of roll. Spread one slice with grain mustard and cover with the halved sausages, tomato and lettuce leaves. Spread mayonnaise on the second slice of bread or half of roll and cover the sandwich.*

## CHICKEN, HAM AND CHEESE

- 1-2 rashers streaky bacon
- 1 15-cm/6-in piece of French stick
- Butter
- 25 g/1 oz cooked chicken, diced
- 25 g/1 oz ham, diced
- 1-2 thin green pepper rings
- 1 teaspoonful finely chopped celery
- 1-2 thin onion rings
- 25 g/1 oz Blue cheese, grated
- Salt and freshly ground black pepper
- 1 dessertspoonful mayonnaise
- 1-2 crisp lettuce leaves
- Grain mustard

*Remove the rinds from the bacon and cook it crisply. Drain well. Cut the French stick in half and butter each slice. Mix the chicken, ham, green pepper, celery, onion, Blue cheese and seasoning together in the mayonnaise to give a fairly moist consistency. Pile this mixture onto the first slice of stick and spread evenly. Cover the mixture with the bacon and lettuce leaves. Spread mustard onto the second slice of stick and cover the sandwich.*

## SALAMI AND CHICKEN

- 2 slices of bread
- Butter
- 1-2 slices of salami
- 1 dessertspoonful chopped cooked chicken
- 1 teaspoonful finely chopped onion
- 1 dessertspoonful grated cheese
- ½ tomato, sliced
- Salt and freshly ground black pepper
- 1-2 crisp lettuce leaves
- Mayonnaise

Butter both slices of bread. Place the salami on one slice and top with the chicken, onion, cheese and tomato. Season to taste and cover with the lettuce. Spread mayonnaise on the second slice of bread and cover the sandwich.

## TURKEY AND GAMMON

- 2 slices of bread
- Butter
- French mustard
- 1 thickish slice cooked gammon
- 1 dessertspoonful pineapple, crushed
- 1-2 slices cooked turkey breast
- 1 teaspoonful cranberry sauce
- Salt and freshly ground black pepper
- 1-2 crisp lettuce leaves
- 25 g/1 oz cream cheese, softened

Butter both slices of bread and spread the first slice with mustard. Top with the gammon, pineapple and turkey breast. Cover with the cranberry sauce, season to taste and top with the lettuce leaves. Spread cream cheese on the second slice of bread and cover the sandwich.

## DUCK WITH STUFFING

- 2 slices of bread
- Butter
- 2 thick slices of roast duck breast
- 1 heaped teaspoonful apple sauce
- 25 g/1 oz sage, onion, parsley and onion stuffing
- Salt and freshly ground black pepper
- 4-5 thin slices of cucumber
- 1-2 crisp lettuce leaves
- Mayonnaise

Butter both slices of bread. Arrange the duck breast evenly on one slice of bread. Spread the apple sauce on top and then the stuffing. Season to taste, then add the cucumber and the lettuce leaves. Spread the second slice of bread with a thin coating of mayonnaise and cover the sandwich.

## PHEASANT WITH CHICKEN LIVER

- 1 rasher streaky bacon
- 2 slices of bread
- Butter
- 2-3 slices cooked pheasant breast
- 1-2 chicken livers, cooked and mashed
- Salt and freshly ground black pepper
- 1 sprig of watercress
- 1-2 crisp lettuce leaves
- Mayonnaise

Remove the rinds from the bacon and cook it crisply. Drain well. Butter both slices of bread. Place the pheasant meat on one slice and cover with the chicken livers and bacon. Season to taste and top with the watercress and lettuce. Spread the second slice of bread with mayonnaise and cover the sandwich.

## VENISON AND CRANBERRY SAUCE

- 1-2 rashers streaky bacon
- 2 slices of bread
- Butter
- 1-2 slices roast venison
- 1 teaspoonful cranberry sauce
- 1-2 sprigs of watercress
- Salt and freshly ground black pepper
- 1-2 crisp lettuce leaves
- Mayonnaise

Remove the rinds from the bacon and cook it crisply. Butter both slices of bread. Lay the venison on one slice and top with the cranberry sauce. Cover with the bacon and the watercress. Season with salt and pepper. Cover with the lettuce. Spread the second slice of bread with mayonnaise and cover the sandwich.

## BRUNCH SANDWICH

- 1-2 rashers streaky bacon
- 1 15-cm/6-in piece of French stick
- Butter
- English or grain mustard
- 1 herby pork sausage, cooked and halved lengthways
- 1 hardboiled egg, mashed
- 1 dessertspoonful mayonnaise
- 1-2 flat mushrooms, cooked
- ½ tomato, sliced
- 1-2 good slices mature Cheddar cheese
- Salt and freshly ground black pepper
- 1-2 crisp lettuce leaves
- Tomato ketchup

Remove the rinds from the bacon and crisply cook it. Drain well. Cut the French stick in half and butter each slice. Spread mustard on the first slice and cover with the sausage and bacon. Mash the egg with the mayonnaise and spread over the sausage and bacon. Top with the mushrooms, tomato and cheese, season to taste and top with lettuce leaves. Spread tomato ketchup on the second slice of bread and cover the sandwich.

## SALAMI, COLESLAW AND BLUE CHEESE

- 1 15-cm/6-in piece of French stick
- Butter
- 25 g/1 oz Blue cheese, crumbled
- 2-3 slices Danish or Italian salami
- 1 dessertspoonful coleslaw
- 1 dessertspoonful beansprouts
- Salt and freshly ground black pepper
- 1-2 crisp lettuce leaves

Cut the French stick in half and butter each side. Spread the Blue cheese on one slice, top with the salami, coleslaw, beansprouts and season to taste. Top with the lettuce leaves and cover with the second slice of bread.

## CRABMEAT WITH BEANSPROUTS

- 2 slices of bread
- Butter
- 25 g/1 oz crabmeat, either fresh or frozen
- 1 hardboiled egg, chopped
- 1 dessertspoonful beansprouts
- A pinch of celery salt
- 1-2 pimento rings, thinly sliced
- A dash of Worcestershire sauce
- A dash of lemon juice
- Salt and freshly ground black pepper
- 1-2 crisp lettuce leaves

Butter both slices of bread. Flake the crabmeat. Mix together the crabmeat, egg, beansprouts, celery salt, pimento, Worcestershire sauce, lemon juice, salt and pepper to a fairly moist consistency. Spread thickly onto one slice of bread and top with the lettuce leaves. Cover with the second slice of bread.

## TUNA FISH AND EGG

- 2 slices of bread
- Butter
- 1 tablespoonful tinned tuna fish, well drained
- 1 teaspoonful finely chopped parsley
- 1/2 teaspoonful finely chopped capers
- 1/4 clove of garlic, crushed
- Salt and freshy ground black pepper
- 1 dessertspoonful mayonnaise
- 1 hardboiled egg, sliced
- 2-3 thin slices of cucumber

Butter both slices of bread. Mix the tuna fish, parsley, capers, garlic and seasoning with the mayonnaise. Heap this mixture onto one slice of bread and top with the egg and cucumber. Cover with the second slice of bread.

# And so to Bed

This And So To Bed chapter has had a chequered career. The first suggestion had been for me to strip down to my nightie and recline à la Elinor Glyn on a sumptuous set of satin sheets. No one had seen the state of my nightie when they suggested that! I favour flanelette whatever the weather. And bed socks. And a woolly hat worn like a tea-cosy, for further comfort. In fact, when I retire for the night all on my ownsome I am the ultimate in visual 'turn-offs'. In short, I could never convince as a sex-symbol. I offered to do it in a jokey way. Take my teeth out (once I get going there's no keeping them in) and doss down on a park bench like a little old bag-lady. But that suggestion was shouted down, I can't begin to think why. I was told to stop being silly, when I was perfectly serious. Being silly is serious. I would hope to claim that I've spent my entire life being silly, and by dressing up as a down-and-out (one of my baser ambitions, to be that). I'd be doing my favourite thing – dressing-up. I'm well known for that in my family.

It doesn't always come off in the way I intend, and has rarely ended by me being the belle-of-the-ball. Indeed, one New Years' Eve, quite the reverse. I ended up trailing home all on my ownsome, my date having chosen to escort back a positive pig-bitch of a blonde who'd come dressed as Cinderella (yuk!), **after** she'd met Prince Charming, of course. Unfortunately for me, my boyfriend had donned a proper Prince Charming outfit (**what** a pair of pins – I'd had no idea that they'd been lurking all the time beneath his cords!). And I do concede that the two of them looked, well – kind of passable together. Whilst he and I looked pretty incongruous, to say the least.

I'd come as a hospital patient, it has to be explained. Swathed from top to toe in grubby bandages, with just the right amount of Heinz Tomato Ketchup oozing from the mouth . . . So convincing did I look that whilst waiting at the bus-stop to go to the ball, an anxious passer-by offered to ring for an ambulance. I won first prize. And wasn't asked to dance once, nor did anyone offer me a drink. Presuming, I suppose, that I was on antibiotics and not allowed to mix them with alcohol. I could think of no other reason at the time. I saw the New Year in on the lavatory, in tears, changing my Tampax. At least it was something of my own to walk home with.

I asked a supporter of silliness to sit, or rather to lie, for our snap. Lovely, loopy, Brenda from The Chelsea Art Club. Brenda is in charge of the bar there and certainly one of the reasons why the Chelsea Arts is so precious to its off-centre members. She also runs her own old-clothes stall every Saturday, in Paddington's Church Street Market. A devastatingly tempting source of dressing-up clothes. 'What sort of sandwich will you be giving me to eat?' She giggled with glee before we'd even begun. 'Hold on,' I was applying scarlet lipstick to her nose at the time, to give that extra touch of authenticity. The effects of over-imbibing and wind-bite. 'A sweet sandwich,' I answered as soon as I'd finished. 'What the hell's a **sweet** sandwich? I was hoping for something with ham.'

But a sweet sandwich was what she got. Marshmallow, whipped cream and chocolate flakes. Children **adore** it – so, incidentally, do I. As would the little old bag-lady I once stopped to give cash to on the Bayswater Road once. 'Here's something for a cup of tea, love.' I cringed at the inevitable condescension of my act, whilst she stared belligerently at my pound note and then glared up at me. 'I don't want no cups of tea!' 'Well, then, a nice drink of whatever you do want.' I stood my ground, the flaming Good Samaritan. 'Don't want no drink neither. But . . .' Her eye brightened. 'I could have a big cake. A big birthday cake to take to bed an' eat all to meself.' 'Do that, then.' I grinned, immensely cheered. She grinned (no teeth) back at me. Yes, she **would** have enjoyed our sweet sandwich.

## MARSHMALLOWS IN HONEY AND GINGER

- 3-4 marshmallows
- 1 tablespoonful clear honey
- 1/4 teaspoonful ground ginger
- 2 slices of wholemeal bread
- Butter
- 1 dessertspoonful whipped cream
- A few chocolate flakes

Marinate the marshmallows in the honey and ginger for 24 hours. Then mash them together. Butter both slices of bread. Spread the mashed marshmallow mixture on one slice and top with the cream and chocolate flakes. Cover with the second slice of bread.

## PASSION FRUIT AND GINSENG

- 1 soft white bap
- Butter
- 2 passion fruit
- 1 tablespoonful thickly whipped cream
- A good pinch of ginseng
- A sprinkling of light brown sugar

Cut the bap in half and butter both halves. Cut the passion fruit in half and remove the seeds and juice. Spread one half of the bap with the cream and cover with the halves of passion fruit. Sprinkle with the ginseng and sugar. Cover with the second half of bap.

## PEANUTS IN WHITE RUM

- 1-2 tablespoonfuls shelled peanuts
- White rum
- 2 slices of wholemeal bread
- Butter
- 1 dessertspoonful crunchy peanut butter
- 1/2 banana, peeled
- 1 small teaspoonful demerara sugar
- 1 teaspoonful whipped double cream

Marinate the peanuts for one week in white rum. Butter both slices of bread. Drain the peanuts and mash them with the peanut butter. Spread the mixture onto one slice of bread. Mash the banana with the demerara sugar and cream and spread on top of the peanut mixture. Cover with the second slice of bread.

# INDEX


almonds
  Chocolate spread with ground almonds 30
  Cream cheese with nuts and fruit 60
anchovy
  Anchovy fillets and olives 75
  Crabmeat and anchovy 38
  Creamed tuna and anchovy 83
apples
  Gouda and apples with walnuts 39
  Liver sausage and apple 36
  Savoury Cheddar with apple 61
  Tongue with apple and red cabbage 37
apricot
  Roast lamb and apricot 42
artichokes
  Mozzarella, artichokes and salami 39
asparagus
  Liver, pimentos and asparagus 51
avocado 61
  Avocado with Roquefort 55
  Chicken and avocado 35
  Chilli-con-carne and avocado 86
  Prawns and avocado 55
  Tuna, avocado and lumpa fish 38
  Turkey and avocado 79

bacon
  Bacon and mushroom 37
  Bacon with mushrooms 87
  Bacon with prunes 81
  Baked beans, egg and bacon 27
  Chicken livers and bacon 69
  Garlic shrimps with bacon and cheese 71
  Grilled cod's roe and bacon 71
  Hot dog, cheese and bacon 67
  Mackerel and cheese with bacon 82
  Sausages, beans and bacon 27
  Spinach, bacon and beans 81
  Turkey, bacon and Gruyère 69
Baked beans, egg and bacon 27
bananas
  Banana and marshmallows 31
  Date and banana 31
  Fried banana and brown sugar 31
  Mashed banana and ginger jam 63
baps 14, 16
beans
  Leeks, beans and carrots 62
  Sausages, beans and bacon 27
  Spinach, bacon and beans 81
beansprouts
  Crabmeat with beansprouts 91
beef 19, 20, 22
  Fillet steak 50
  Rare beef with horseradish 50
  Roast beef with cheese 43
  Salt beef 43 see also Corned beef, and Hamburgers
Blue cheese with black grapes 59
bread 13-18
  recipes 15-17
  storing, freezing 15
Brunch sandwich 90
butter, buttering 21

cabbage
  Pork and red cabbage 87
  Tongue with apple and red cabbage 37
carrot
  Cottage cheese and carrot 60
  Leeks, beans and carrots 62
carving and slicing 22
celery
  Pork with celery and Mozzarella 44
cheese 19
  Avocado with Roquefort 55
  Blue cheese with black grapes 59
  Cheese and crackers 29
  Chicken and Cheddar 79
  Chicken, ham and cheese 88
  Chicken, spinach, tomato and cheese 44
  Cottage cheese and carrot 60
  Cottage cheese with walnuts 47
  Crab and Parmesan cheese 83
  Cream cheese and chives 59
  Cream cheese with nuts and fruit 60
  Emmenthal cheese and green peppers 47
  Fish with Roquefort or Blue cheese 39
  Frankfurters and cheese 82
  Gammon and mushroom with cheese 36
  Garlic shrimps with bacon and cheese 71
  Goat cheese with cucumber 60
  Gouda and apples with walnuts 39
  Gruyère and pineapple 47
  Ham, cheese and pickle salad 68
  Hamburger and Blue cheese 51
  Hot dog, cheese and bacon 67
  Mackerel and cheese with bacon 82
  Mozzarella, artichokes and salami 39
  Pork with celery and Mozzarella 44
  Roast beef with cheese 43
  Salami, coleslaw and Blue cheese 91
  Salmon and cream cheese 45
  Savoury Cheddar with apple 61
  Smoked haddock in cheese 54
  Turkey and Blue cheese 78
  Turkey, bacon and Gruyère 69
  Welsh rarebit 61
chicken 18-19, 20, 22
  Chicken and avocado 35
  Chicken and Cheddar 79
  Chicken, ham and cheese 88
  Chicken livers and bacon 69
  Chicken salad 68
  Chicken, spinach, tomato and cheese 44
  Creamed chicken and ham 29
  Ham with chicken livers 80
  Hot curried chicken 34
  Pheasant with chicken liver 90
  Salami and chicken 89
Chilli-con-carne and avocado 86
chocolate
  Chocolate, honey and nuts 30
  Chocolate spread with ground almonds 30
  Chocolate surprise 30
cod's roe
  Grilled cod's roe and bacon 71
coleslaw
  Frankfurters and coleslaw 66
  Hamburger with Frankfurters and coleslaw 28
  Salami, coleslaw and Blue cheese 91
Corned beef and horseradish sauce 67
Corned beef hash 68
Cornish cream tea 75
Cottage cheese and carrot 60
Cottage cheese with walnuts 47
Crab 54
  Crab and Parmesan cheese 83
  Crabmeat and mushrooms 83
  Crabmeat and anchovy 38
  Crabmeat with beansprouts 91
Cream cheese and chives 59
Cream cheese with nuts and fruit 60
Creamed chicken and ham 29
Creamed tuna and anchovy 83
Cucumber 74
  Goat cheese with cucumber 60
Cumberland sausages with tomato 88
Curried egg salad 58

dates
  Date and banana 31
  Ginger, walnuts and dates 63
Devilled turkey 35
duck 18-19, 20, 22
  Duck in port with green olives 52
  Duck with pineapple and honey 53
  Duck with stuffing 89
  Duck with sweet and sour sauce 78

eggs 19
  Baked beans, egg and bacon 27
  Curried egg salad 58
  Egg and mushroom 58
  Egg with spinach and garlic 45
  Sardine and egg 27
  Scrambled egg and marmite 29
  Tongue and egg salad 28
  Tuna fish and egg 91
Emmenthal cheese and green peppers 47

Fillet steak 50
fish 18-19
  Fish with Roquefort or Blue cheese 39
frankfurters
  Frankfurters and cheese 82
  Frankfurters and coleslaw 66
  Hamburger wirh Frankfurters and coleslaw 28
  Hot dog, cheese and bacon 67
Fried banana and brown sugar 31
fruit
  Cream cheese with nuts and fruit 60

gammon
  Gammon and mushroom with cheese 36
  Gammon and pineapple 80
  Gammon with potato salad and honey 88
  Turkey and gammon 89
Gannet's special 44
Garlic prawns 38
Garlic shrimps with bacon and cheese 71
Gentleman's relish with mushrooms 75
Ginger, walnuts and dates 63

Goat cheese with cucumber 60
Gouda and apples with walnuts 39
granary bread 14, 17
grapes
Blue cheese with black grapes 59
Pheasant with black grapes 53
grilled or oven-cooked sandwiches 22, 23
Baked beans, egg and bacon 27
Corned beef hash 68
Fillet steak 50
Grilled cod's roe and bacon 71
Hamburgers and Blue cheese 51
Hot dog, cheese and bacon 67
Gruyère and pineapple 47

haddock
Smoked haddock in cheese 54
Smoked haddock with horseradish 45
ham 20, 22
Chicken, ham and cheese 88
Creamed chicken and ham 29
Ham and peach chutney 52
Ham, cheese and pickle salad 68
Ham with chicken livers 80
Ham with pears 80
Ham with vegetables 43
Parma ham and melon 51
Hamburger and Blue cheese 51
Hamburger in sesame seed roll 67
Hamburgers with Frankfurters and coleslaw 28
hazelnuts
Chocolate, honey and nuts 30
Herby bread 16-17
honey
Chocolate, honey and nuts 30
Duck with pineapple and honey 53
Gammon with potato salad and honey 88
Marshmallows in honey and ginger 94
Hot curried chicken 34
Hot dog, cheese and bacon 67
hot sandwiches see grilled or oven-cooked and toasted
Humous in pitta bread 70

ingredients: buying and preparation 18-20, 22
Instant breakfast rolls 16
Italian special 59

jam
Cornish cream tea 75
Mashed banana and ginger jam 63
Peanut butter and strawberry jam 26
Raspberry jam with hundreds and thousands 30

lamb 18-19, 22
Lamb with spinach and peach chutney 86
Roast lamb and apricot 42
Roast lamb and jelly 42
Leeks, beans and carrots 62
Liver, pimentos and asparagus 51
Liver sausage and apple 36
lumpa fish
Tuna, avocado and lumpa fish 38

Mackerel and cheese with bacon 82
marmite
Scrambled egg and marmite 29
marshmallows
Banana and marshmallows 31
Marshmallows in honey and ginger 94
Mashed banana and ginger jam 63
melon
Parma ham and melon 51
Mozzarella, artichokes and salami 39
mushrooms
Bacon and mushroom 37
Bacon with mushrooms 87
Crabmeat and mushrooms 83
Egg and mushroom 58
Gammon and mushroom with cheese 36
Gentleman's relish with mushrooms 75
Mushrooms with soured cream 62
Savoury sardine and mushroom 74
Spinach, mushrooms and garlic 62
Mussels with savoury paste 55

nuts see almonds; hazelnuts; peanuts; and walnuts

olives
Anchovy fillets and olives 75
Duck in port with green olives 52
open sandwiches 23
oven-cooked sandwiches see grilled or oven-cooked

Parma ham and melon 51
Passion fruit and ginseng 94
Peanut butter 26
Peanut butter and pineapple 26
Peanut butter and strawberry jam 26
Peanuts in white rum 94
pears
Ham with pears 80
peppers
Emmenthal cheese and green peppers 47
pheasant 18-19, 20, 22
Pheasant with black grapes 53
Pheasant with chestnut stuffing 53
Pheasant with chicken liver 90
pimentos
Liver, pimentos and asparagus 51
pineapple
Duck with pineapple and honey 53
Gammon and pineapple 80
Gruyère and pineapple 47
Peanut butter and pineapple 26
pitta bread 15, 17, 69, 70
pork 19-20, 22
Pork and apple sauce 79
Pork and pickled onion 87
Pork and red cabbage 87
Pork with celery and Mozzarella 44
prawns
Garlic prawns 38
Prawns and avocado 55
prunes
Bacon with prunes 81

Rare beef with horseradish 50
Raspberry jam with hundreds and thousands 30
Roast beef with cheese 43
Roast lamb and apricot 42
Roast lamb and jelly 42
Rollmops 37
Russian salad 63

Salads 18, 23
Chicken salad 68
Curried egg salad 58
Gammon with potato salad and honey 88
Ham, cheese and pickle salad 68
Italian special 59
Russian salad 63
Tongue and egg salad 23
salami
Mozzarella, artichokes and salami 39
Salami and chicken 89
Salami, coleslaw and Blue cheese 91
salmon
Salmon and cream cheese 45
Salmon fish cakes 70
Smoked salmon 75
Salmon trout with hollandaise 82
Salt beef 43
sardines
Sardine and egg 27
Savoury sardine and mushroom 74
Spicy sardine 46
Sausages, beans and bacon 27
Savoury Cheddar with apple 61
Savoury sardine and mushroom 74
Scrambled egg and marmite 29
Seafood special 46
shrimps
Garlic shrimps with bacon and cheese 71
Shrimp and tuna cocktail 54
slicing and carving 22
Smoked salmon 75
spinach
Chicken, spinach, tomato and cheese 44
Egg with spinach and garlic 45
Lamb with spinach and peach chutney 86
Spinach, bacon and beans 81
Spinach, mushrooms and garlic 62
Tongue and spinach 81

toasted sandwiches 22, 23
Avocado 61
Chicken livers and bacon 69
Corned beef and horseradish sauce 67
Gammon and mushroom with cheese 36
Garlic shrimps with bacon and cheese 71
Hamburger in sesame seed roll 67
Hamburger with Frankfurters and coleslaw 28
Roast beef with cheese 43
Sausages, beans and bacon 27
Spinach, bacon and beans 81
Turkey and Blue cheese 78
Welsh rarebit 61
tomato
Chicken, spinach, tomato and cheese 44
Cumberland sausages with tomato 88
Tongue 19, 22
Tongue and egg salad 28
Tongue and spinach 81
Tongue with apple and red cabbage 37
tuna
Creamed tuna and anchovy 83
Shrimp and tuna cocktail 54
Tuna, avocado and lumpa fish 38
Tuna fish and egg 91
turkey 18-19, 20, 22
Devilled turkey 35
Turkey and avocado 79
Turkey and Blue cheese 78
Turkey and cranberry sauce 35
Turkey and gammon 89
Turkey, bacon and Gruyère 69
Turkey with savoury paste 52

Venison and cranberry sauce 90

walnuts
Cottage cheese with walnuts 47
Ginger, walnuts and dates 63
Gouda and apples with walnuts 39
Welsh rarebit 61

yeast 13